The Age of Revolution

D1672990

Charles Kovacs

The Age of Revolution

Waldorf Education Resources

Floris Books

First published in volume form in 2003
Second printing 2014

© 2003 Estate of Charles Kovacs

British Library CIP Data available

ISBN 978-086315-395-2

Printed in Poland

Contents

The Nineteenth and Twentieth Centuries

Foreword

Charles Kovacs was a teacher at the Rudolf Steiner School in Edinburgh for many years. The Waldorf/Steiner schools sprang from the pedagogical ideas and insights of the Austrian philosopher Rudolf Steiner (1864–1925). The curriculum aims to awaken much more than merely the intellectual development—it seeks to educate the whole being of the growing child, that each may develop their full human and spiritual potential.

During his time as a teacher Charles Kovacs wrote extensive notes of his lessons day by day. Since then these texts have been used and appreciated by teachers in Edinburgh and other Waldorf/Steiner schools for many years. This book represents the way one teacher taught a particular group of children, other teachers will find their own way of presenting the material. While some of the detail in this book, such as the endless wars between Scotland and England, may not be relevant in teaching history today in other countries, what is nevertheless interesting is how Kovacs picks out pertinent stories for the context in which he was teaching, and creates a tapestry showing the development of humankind from medieval times, when every person had their place in the hierarchy of society, to the awakening of individuality in modern times.

In editing the present text, dates have been checked, but it has not been possible to verify every story that Kovacs found in his extensive reading (largely in his local public library). The last two chapters have been more extensively edited to bring them up to date.

Astrid Maclean
Edinburgh 2003

Rebellions

1. Spain and Holland

The most important thing we learn from history is to see that the human mind, the human soul are not always the same — they change in the course of history, in the course of centuries. You all here are different today from what you were six or seven years ago, not only in your body but in your mind, you have grown mentally as well as with your body. And just as we grow up individually, so mankind as a whole is growing up. And the story of mankind's growing up is called history.

Now think back to the early medieval times, when the peasants, the villains and serfs, looked up with great respect to their lords and master, the knights, and the knights respected and obeyed their master, the kings. And they all, peasants, knights, kings, looked with great respect upon monks and priests, the holy servants of God. The monks and priests were not only respected as holy men, they were also respected because they could read and write, they had all the knowledge there was in books. And the monks and priests looked up to their masters, the bishops: and the bishops respected and obeyed their lord, the Pope in Rome. All this was about a thousand years ago — that's about thirty generations ago. If you look back to that time thirty generations ago, one could say it was the time of *authority;* everybody had a "higher authority" over him — and the highest authority over all was the Pope in Rome.

It may sound quite strange to us, that even if a king was stupid or evil, his knights would still obey him; even if a monk behaved not at all like a holy man, he would still be respected; and no matter what kind of person the Pope was, he was still the highest authority to whom all looked up with great reverence. The people in those days wanted an authority over them, deep down they liked it that there was somebody who told them what they should do and what they should think.

And the people — the few people — who wanted to think

for themselves and who came to ideas which the Pope and bishops did not like, these people were called "heretics." And they had a very bad time. There was a special court of justice, called the *Inquisition*. It was not an ordinary court of judges and lawyers, it was a court of priests and bishops, and the poor heretics who came before this court were nearly always condemned to death and burnt at the stake. The bishops and priests who condemned Joan of Arc to death were such a court of the dreadful Inquisition.

You see, the Inquisition was just a part of this time of authority; most people in the world wanted to have an authority over them, and anybody who challenged the authority — specially the authority of the Church, the authority of the Pope — just had to be killed because they upset the authority which all the other people wanted.

All that was about a thousand years ago, and it lasted for about five hundred years. Then around five hundred years ago there came this great change in the human soul — the age of discoveries, the age of inventions. Now there were more than a few isolated heretics — thousands and millions of people everywhere in Europe began to think for themselves.

And as people began to think for themselves, they not only made voyages into unknown seas, they not only looked at the stars through telescopes (as Galileo Galilei did), they were also no longer willing to bow down before authority.

Luther could call the Pope a scoundrel and a devil, and the Pope could do nothing against him, for hundreds of thousands of Germans were willing to fight for Luther and defend him. Thus came the Reformation: it came in Germany, in England, in Scotland. People did not want the authority of the Pope any longer, at least in the northern countries of Europe. In the South, in Italy, in Spain, people remained Roman Catholic, they wanted the authority of the Pope — and Spain, Portugal and Italy have remained Roman Catholic to this day.

But there were also countries where the people had to fight a long and terrible struggle to free themselves from the authority of the Pope. Such a country was Holland.

Now at that time, five hundred years ago, Holland was not a

country on its own — it was a part of Germany. And as the Reformation spread through Germany it also reached Holland and many of the Dutch people became Protestants. The emperor of Germany and many other lands at that time was Charles V, a mighty ruler. He ruled Germany, Austria, Spain, and the Spanish colonies in America. People said: "In his empire the sun never sets." Charles V was a very devout Roman Catholic, but he did not want any bloodshed in his lands and so he did nothing to stop people from becoming Protestants. He did not like it by any means, however, he did not want the people he ruled to suffer violence and bloodshed. But all this changed when Charles V died in 1558.

Upon the death of this mighty ruler his great empire was divided between his two sons. One son ruled over Germany and Austria, the other over Spain and the Spanish colonies in America, as well as Holland.

It is rather strange that Holland — which was so close to Germany — should have come under the rule of a Spanish king, thousands of miles away, but that is how the empire of Charles V was divided. And so the Dutch came under the rule of Spain. The son of Charles V who inherited Spain and also Holland was Philip II. He was the king who sent the great Armada against England and suffered a terrible defeat. But of course the battle of the little English ships against the Armada happened much later.

What happened first, many years before the Armada, was that Philip II, the King of Spain, was also ruler of Holland. But Philip was not like his father, he was a fanatical Roman Catholic. He would not allow Protestants in any country under his dominion, and he was determined to make an end of the Protestants in Holland.

Philip II did not bother to go to Holland himself to suppress the Dutch Protestants — he gave the task to a woman, to his half-sister Margaret. She was appointed Governor of Holland, and given the task to destroy the Dutch Protestants.

And so the dreaded Inquisition came to Holland, these courts of law which did not deal with ordinary crimes but only with "crimes against the Roman Church." The Dutch

Protestants were dragged before the Inquisition, tortured, condemned to death and then burnt at the stake.

Now there were also a good many Roman Catholics in Holland, people who had nothing to fear from the horrors of the Inquisition — but they could not stand seeing their compatriots, their fellow-Dutchmen, tortured and burnt to death. In particular there were two Dutch noblemen who were devout Roman Catholics but who felt that Margaret, the Governor, was going too far. The names of these two noblemen were William of Orange, and Egmont. They went to Margaret and begged her — on behalf of all Dutch Roman Catholics — to stop the Inquisition and its horrors.

Now Margaret was a very cunning woman; she realized that if she did not pay attention to William of Orange and Egmont, there was a chance that the Dutch Catholics and Protestants would join together and rise against her and against the Spanish rule altogether. She did not have enough soldiers at her command to fight the whole Dutch nation, so Margaret pretended that she would do what William and Egmont asked for, and the Inquisition was stopped.

The Dutch people were overjoyed: whenever William and Egmont went in the streets of Dutch cities, people cheered them and blessed them. They all thought the bad times of persecution and terror were over. But while the Dutch were jubilant, believing all was well, Margaret had more and more soldiers sent from Spain (they had to come by sea) until she had an army, so large that it could crush any Dutch resistance.

At this point something happened that gave Margaret the excuse she needed. There were many beautiful old churches in Holland — they had been built in the past when all the people were Roman Catholics, when all accepted the authority of the Pope. The Roman Catholics had all these churches, but the new faith, the Protestants had no churches for themselves. In some places the Protestants decided that this was not fair, so they stormed the churches and threw the Catholics out.

Margaret was very pleased when this happened — this was the excuse for which she had waited, the excuse to bring back the Inquisition, the excuse to use her great army if the Dutch tried to resist. But Margaret was very cunning. She first called all the Dutch Catholic noblemen together, amongst them William of Orange and Egmont. And she said: "You see what happened when I stopped the Inquisition, how the Protestants are attacking us, the Catholics, driving us out of our churches. So the Inquisition has to come back. What I demand from you as good Roman Catholics is an oath of loyalty — that you will stand by me and help me destroy the Protestants."

Egmont and many other Dutch nobles swore this oath of loyalty; but William of Orange did not trust the Spanish and their trickery, he was certain that even if he swore that oath, his life would not be safe. He also spoke to his friend, Egmont, saying: "Margaret hates both of us because we made her stop the Inquisition. She will not be satisfied until we have paid with our lives for it. I am going to flee to Germany before she strikes at us. Come with me."

But Egmont would not listen to him. He trusted Margaret, he trusted King Philip II. And so William of Orange bade farewell to Egmont, and knew in his heart he would never see his friend again. He then fled to Germany.

Now that Margaret had made certain that the Dutch Catholics would not stand in her way, now that she had a large army of Spanish soldiers at her command, she started to deal with the Protestants.

First of all, the Dutch Protestants were told they had twenty-four hours to leave the country: any Protestant found in Holland after that time could expect no mercy. You can imagine what happened: people quickly packing as much as they could and carrying it on their backs — the roads of Holland all crammed with refugees, some fleeing to Germany but many also getting into boats to take them to England.

Throughout British history, the British have often benefited from letting refugees come to their land. The Dutch were famous for their skills in weaving cloth, they brought their skill and knowledge to Britain, starting the textile industries, the weaving of woollen cloth, which until recently, was one of the great and very profitable industries in Yorkshire and Scotland. It was the Dutch Protestants fleeing from the

Inquisition who helped to make these into great and flourishing industries.

But only a small part of the Dutch Protestants could save themselves. Many of them were too poor to pay for a passage to England, others did not want to leave their homeland even if their lives were at stake — and many stayed in the hope that Margaret would only punish the men who had stormed the Catholic churches, and that innocent people who had not harmed anybody had nothing to fear.

Well, Margaret certainly punished those, they were found out and hanged by the hundreds. Perhaps Margaret would have been quite willing to leave it at that and do no more against the Protestants. But now her half-brother and master, King Philip II of Spain, decided that a woman was, perhaps, too soft-hearted to wipe out the Dutch Protestants, so he sent a man to Holland, a Spanish nobleman, the Duke of Alba. He was the right man for this task: haughty and proud, utterly without mercy, and a man who regarded anybody who was not Spanish and not Roman Catholic as a kind of animal that could be killed as one kills rats or other vermin. When the Duke of Alba arrived in Holland there began a time of terror, of bloodshed and torture such as Holland had never known before.

Yet, as we shall see, it was this terror and oppression which roused the Dutch people against their cruel Spanish rulers.

2. The Dutch Rebellion

The Dutch Catholic noblemen had sworn an oath of loyalty and support for Margaret — even the noble Egmont had sworn this oath. Only William of Orange had refused — and had fled to Germany. And now the Duke of Alba arrived in Holland with special instructions from King Philip II about how to deal with the Dutch people. Shortly after his arrival, Alba invited the noblemen to a banquet. Egmont was also invited and came, but when the banquet was finished and Egmont was leaving, he was stopped at the door by soldiers who took him away and threw him into prison.

On the same day Spanish soldiers were put on guard in every part of Holland to stop any more Dutch from fleeing. From now on it was a crime punishable by death to try and leave the country.

Then Duke Alba set up courts which were far worse than the Inquisition, the Dutch called them Blood Courts. The Spanish Judges in these courts had a very simple rule: a Dutchman was guilty of high treason against His Majesty the King of Spain if he had ever listened to a Protestant preacher, or if he had a friend or relative who was a Protestant, or if he had a friend or relation who had fled from Holland, or if he had ever made a remark against the King of Spain.

This meant of course that every person in Holland was guilty under that law. But, as Alba had made it known, if he did not have all Dutch people killed, those who stayed alive owed this only to Alba's kindness and generosity — they had not deserved it!

And so these so-called "judges" began their work. One of the first to be tried and condemned to death was Egmont. All his life he had been a good Roman Catholic, a loyal, faithful supporter of King Philip II — but this did not save him. In 1568 he was beheaded and his head put on a spike to show the Dutch what was in store for them. Perhaps in his last moments Egmont remembered the warning of his friend, William of Orange.

But Egmont was only the first of countless others who lost their lives. There was not a day in any city of Holland when there were no executions. Merchants, teachers, doctors could be seen, tied to horses' tails and dragged to the gallows or the stake or the executioner's block. No one knew in the morning if he would still be free or alive at nightfall.

However, under this rule of terror, there grew amongst the Dutch people the will and the resolution to rise and fight against the cruel Spanish oppressors. All they needed was a leader, a general, experienced in war and battles, a man of courage and determination. And such a man came: it was William of Orange.

He returned to Holland in secret, and soon had a little band of desperate men. They knew they had only a small chance against the great might of Spain, but they would rather die fighting than be hanged like criminals or burnt at the stake.

When this little army attacked a Spanish camp here, and another one there, the Spaniards were at first taken completely by surprise, and William of Orange conquered a few Dutch towns where the people received him with joy.

But after the first shock of surprise, the well-trained Spanish soldiers soon had their regiments in fighting order, and William's small force could not stand up to the Spanish army — it had to retreat from the towns it had taken. The Spaniards — in their thirst for revenge — killed all the inhabitants, men, women and children in these unhappy towns.

But now even the Roman Catholics in Holland turned against the cruel Spaniards. In cities and villages Catholics and Protestants joined forces and rose against Alba and his army of butchers. And as soon as Alba quelled a rebellion in one place, another rebellion started somewhere else.

So the rebellion grew and spread — but William had never an army big enough to break the power of Spain. The Spaniards on the other hand could win a battle here and a battle there, but they could never vanquish William and they could not make an end of the rebellion. And so the war dragged on and on.

3. The Siege of Leyden

The most famous action in this war between the Dutch and the Spaniards was the Siege of Leyden in 1574. Leyden was one of those Dutch cities that have been built "at the bottom of the sea," but of course, after the sea had been pushed out by great dikes. The city of Leyden was, therefore, built below sea-level and only the great walls of the dikes kept the sea out.

Like many other Dutch cities, Leyden had declared itself for William of Orange, whereupon a Spanish general called Valdez marched a large army against the city and laid siege to it. General Valdez did not try to take Leyden by storm, he reckoned that sooner or later hunger would force the citizens of Leyden to surrender.

And so weeks passed and months passed: in the city food became scarce and there came great suffering. People killed their cats and dogs and ate them, even rats and mice were eaten. Very young children and very old people died — they did not have enough strength to live on the tiny rations. This was the moment when the cunning Spanish General Valdez sent a messenger to the Mayor of Leyden asking him to surrender the city.

By this time there were quite a number of people in Leyden who had had enough of being ravenously hungry day or night. When they heard a Spanish messenger had arrived, they came together in the great square before the town hall and shouted: "Surrender, surrender!" Some even threatened to kill the Mayor if he would not open the gates to the Spaniards who would at least bring food.

The Mayor came out and walked calmly into the midst of the crowd. And when the people saw him the shouting stopped, and the Mayor began to speak: "It is terrible to suffer the pangs of hunger as we all have done now for weeks — but it is still better than to suffer the inhuman tortures which the cruel Spaniards are going to inflict on you once you are in their

power. I will not surrender my city — and if you want to surrender you have to kill me first. Here is my sword — any one of
you can plunge it into my heart — and then you are free to let
the Spaniards in. But as long as I live I will not surrender, and no
true Dutchman will."

And with these words he drew his sword and held it out to
the crowd. For a moment there was deep silence, and then there
came one great shout: "No surrender!" And the Spanish messenger returned to General Valdez with the news that these mad
Dutchmen would still not surrender. General Valdez only
smiled, another week and they would give in, so he thought.

What the proud Spaniard did not know was that during that
night a man crawled and crept cautiously and silently through
the Spanish lines towards Leyden — the soldiers on guard never
noticed the dark shadow that made its way through the camp.
The man reached Leyden — and brought a message of hope to
the city, a message that put new heart into the people and gave
them new strength.

The messenger who had come from William of Orange told the
burghers of Leyden that a fleet was coming to their rescue, not a
big fleet but large enough to carry plenty of food and also soldiers to help in the fight against the Spaniards. The city of
Leyden — and the fields outside the city where in times of peace
the peasants grew wheat and grazed cows — were protected
against the sea by dikes, and so the ships could only reach
Leyden if the citizens broke the dikes, then the sea-water would
cover the ground and at high tide the ships could sail in to the
rescue and bring food.

It was a sad thing for the people of Leyden to be told that
they would have to break the dikes which their forefathers
had built with so much hard work, it was a sad thing to let the
sea come in and cover fields and meadows; the sea-water
would ruin the soil for years to come and nothing would grow
on it. But the people of Leyden had no choice: they had to use
their old enemy, the sea, against the new enemy, the Spaniards
— otherwise the rescue ships could not reach them. And so
they demolished the dikes and the sea-water poured in and

covered the fields and its waves lapped round the walls of Leyden.

The flooding came as quite a surprise to the Spaniards, the water was rising and coming up to their knees — and they quickly withdrew to two fortresses which stood on higher ground and so remained above water.

But, unfortunately for the Dutch, the water did not rise high enough for the ships. Even when the high tide came it was too shallow for the ships. The people of Leyden looked out from their walls over the waves which now covered the land around the city, they looked out hoping to see the ships William of Orange had sent to their rescue, but the ships remained out in the deep sea. And when night came, the people of Leyden were in dark despair. It seemed as if their last hope had gone, they had sacrificed the fields and farms to no purpose.

But during the night a storm blew up, a roaring gale lashed the North Sea, and great waves swept high over the ruined dikes, the water level rose — and in the howling storm and riding the great waves the Dutch fleet sailed in towards Leyden.

But they did not go very far — for between the high sea and the city of Leyden there was the higher ground with the two Spanish fortresses. And the cannons of the Spaniards could have shattered every Dutch ship before it ever got near Leyden. And so the Dutch sailors dared not go on — they kept their ships out of reach of the Spanish cannons and did not sail on to Leyden.

Just imagine that night: pitch dark, the storm howling, the uproar of the waves — and no one really knowing what was going on. The people of Leyden had already given up all hope, and expected the Spaniards to come at any moment; the Spaniards, on the other hand were also afraid — they had seen the dark shapes of the Dutch ships come in and expected a battle with them at any moment.

And just then, there came a terrific crash, so loud that it could be heard for miles. What had happened was that the surging waves had washed away the foundations under a part of the wall of Leyden and this whole section of the wall came tumbling down.

The people of Leyden, hearing the crash, thought the

Spaniards had blown up the wall — and, as they no longer had the strength to fight — they prepared themselves to die.

But they need not have feared; the Spaniards, too, were frightened by the crash. They thought the noise was caused by the people of Leyden coming to attack them and at the same time the Dutch ships would attack. And the Spaniards had no wish to fight on two sides, the Dutch ships on one side and the people of Leyden on the other side. And so the Spaniards took flight, they left the fortresses and cannons behind, and up to their breasts in water they strode through the flooded country-side to reach dry ground far away from Leyden.

When nothing came the Dutch discovered to their surprise and joy that the fortresses had been abandoned and that there was not a Spaniard in sight. The ships could sail in and bring food to the famished people of Leyden.

The rescue of Leyden was a great event for Holland; messengers on horse-back galloped from town to town to bring the good news* and it made the Dutch people even more determined to fight the Spanish oppressors.

In the end King Philip II of Spain realized that the Duke of Alba with his rule of terror and torture had only united the Dutch, Catholics and Protestants, against Spain. Alba was recalled to Spain in disgrace — even Margaret had to go back to Spain. Now Philip sent one governor after another to win back the Dutch by kind words and promises, but it was in vain. The Dutch did not want to be ruled by Spain any longer; they declared Holland an independent country and offered William of Orange the crown. But William was so modest that he did not want to be called King. So in 1576 Holland became a republic. But a republic must have a president — or as the Dutch called it a "protector" — and the first protector or president, as we would say, was William of Orange.

Philip of Spain was beside himself with rage when he heard of William's election. In his fury he offered a great reward to any man who would murder William of Orange. And in 1584 a vile man, Gérard, tried to earn this reward and stabbed William to

* See Robert Browning's poem "How they brought the good news to Ghent."

death. But he was caught and executed, and the Dutch elected William's son, Maurice of Nassau, as "protector." So Philip gained nothing by the foul murder. Quite the contrary — young Maurice made a treaty of alliance with Queen Elizabeth of England who sent soldiers and arms to Holland to help the Dutch against Spain.

You can imagine the anger of King Philip: he had tried to break the stubborn Dutch by terror and torture — it had not worked; he had tried fine words and promises — they had not listened; he had instigated the murder of their leader, William of Orange — and this had also not made any difference. And now they were becoming allies of his most hated enemies, the English! It was then that Philip decided to build a vast fleet, the Great Armada in order to first conquer Britain and then crush little Holland.

As you know Philip's great Armada was destroyed by the little ships of England and the gales; it was not only a victory for England, it also saved Holland; after the loss of the Armada Philip had to give up all hope of regaining Holland. It remained a free country.

But the fighting in Holland, the soldiers, the arms, the ships of the Armada — all this cost money. In his mad desire to crush the Protestants in Holland and England, Philip spent the vast treasury of gold which the Spaniards had taken with great cruelty from the Indians of Peru and Mexico; all the treasures which had come from America were used up by Philip to pay for his wars.

And when he died, Spain which had been the richest country in Europe, was again as poor as she had been a hundred years earlier, before the discovery of America. But little Holland flourished — through nothing else but their hard work.

So the people of Leyden had not suffered hunger and starvation in vain; their determination, and that of the other Dutch people had in the end defeated the might of Spain and brought it down.

4. The Divine Right of Kings

The story of the rebellion of the Netherlands is a stirring tale of brave men fighting against a mighty and cruel oppressor. But it is also, in one way, a sad tale — for it is a story of Christians fighting each other for the sake of religion.

But it was not only so in the Netherlands; we come now to a time in history when all over Europe Catholics and Protestants fought each other, and then the Protestants began to fight amongst themselves over some difference between one kind of Church and another. You might ask, "How could it be that people who believed in Christ, the Lord of Love, could persecute and kill each other in the name of the Christian religion?" But for centuries people had been used to thinking that a person of another faith, a "heretic" was evil and deserved to be punished: that's what the Pope in Rome had always taught. Now the Protestants had broken away from the Pope, but they still had the old way of thinking and they treated the Roman Catholics as "heretics" as well as any Protestants who had a slightly different kind of worship or Church. It took a long time until this misguided way of thinking disappeared.

When in 1603 Queen Elizabeth of England appointed James VI, the son of Mary Stuart, as her successor, Scotland and England became one country under one ruler, James I of Great Britain as he was thence known.

Now James is a very odd king in English history: he was a Scot of course, and spoke with a strong Scots accent all his life, but the Scots people soon had good reason to hate him. James's mother, Mary Stuart, had been a Roman Catholic, but James had been brought up away from his mother as a Protestant, and the Catholics in Britain soon hated him. After a time a good many Protestants came to hate him too. Few kings in history have managed to make as many enemies as James.

If James had not been brought up as a Protestant, Elizabeth

would never have made him her successor. But there were still quite a number of Roman Catholics in England, and they hoped that the son of Mary Stuart would really, in his heart, be a Roman Catholic and once he was King of England would again make the old religion, that of Rome, the religion of England. But James did nothing of the sort, he had no liking for the Church of Rome at all and showed it. Catholics were not allowed to have churches or to worship in public.

And so the English Roman Catholics regarded James as a traitor, he had "betrayed" his mother's religion. And a number of Roman Catholic noblemen hatched a plot to do away with King James and with the whole English Parliament as well.

The leader of this plot was a man called Guy Fawkes, and the plot is called the "Gunpowder Plot," because the plan was to use gunpowder to blow up the English Parliament and everybody in it on a day when the King was there.

Underneath the houses of Parliament in London, there were big cellars, and merchants — or anybody else — who wanted a store for his goods could rent one of these cellars from the government.

So it was quite easy for Guy Fawkes and his fellow-conspirators to rent one of these cellars, and they carried into it 36 barrels of gunpowder and sticks of fire-wood — and they laid fuses. Now they only had to wait for the day when King James would come and visit the Houses of Parliament, the next date when this was to happen was November 5, 1605. On that day Guy Fawkes himself was to put fire to the fuses.

Now one of the conspirators had a friend who was a courtier of King James and who was to accompany the King when he visited Parliament. The conspirator could not bear to let his friend go to his death — and so he wrote him a letter — in a disguised hand, without signature — warning him not to go to Parliament with the King, as there would be a "great blow."

The courtier was puzzled — he could not imagine what all this was supposed to mean. But something was going to happen in the Parliament, that seemed certain. He took the letter to the King's Chief Minister, Lord Salisbury — who was a very clever man and immediately guessed "great blow" meant an explosion.

And having thought it over, he went with the letter to the King and warned him that there was a plot against his life. Immediately (it was already the night of the 4th November) soldiers were sent to search the cellars under the Parliament, they went from cellar to cellar and found Guy Fawkes laying the fuses amongst the barrels of gunpowder. He was arrested, tortured until he gave the names of the other conspirators, and they were all executed. To this day the event is commemorated every November 5 with fireworks, a bonfire and a "Guy" is burned.

You might think that because he was hated by the Catholics, James would at least have all the Protestants on his side. But it was not so. The Protestants were split into two parties. There was first of all, the Church of England, and James as King, was the head of this Church. But there were also the Puritans (meaning "the pure ones"). The Puritans thought the Church of England was far too much like the Church of Rome, because it allowed statues and paintings and organ-music and candles, and it also had bishops and archbishops. The Puritans hated all this — they called it "popery" and they would not go to such a Church. They had their own prayer meetings without all these things. The Puritans always dressed in dark clothes; they regarded bright colours as sinful. They also regarded theatres and dancing and playing cards — in short all amusements — as sins.

The Puritans did not want to have anything to do with the Church of England. But King James who was head of the Church of England wanted only one kind of Church and one kind of service in his whole kingdom. The Puritans were forbidden to hold their prayer meetings — and those who did were thrown into prison or had to pay heavy fines.

Many Puritans found this persecution so unbearable that, in the end, they bought a ship, called the *Mayflower* and one hundred families sailed on the *Mayflower* to America where they started a new colony called New England. These Puritans were called the Pilgrim Fathers, and the day of their arrival in America, November 11, 1620, is remembered with a national holiday in the United States — Thanksgiving.

So, not only the Catholics, but also the puritan Protestants had no liking for King James. But in Scotland, the Church of Scotland, founded by John Knox, did not want to have bishops or archbishops, and the Scots stubbornly refused to obey King James' wish that their Church should become like the Church of England. So King James had few friends in his native Scotland and most people hated him.

You would think that James had at least won the hearts of the English people who belonged to the Church of England. But he even made ordinary English people his enemies — for a different reason, a reason that had nothing to do with religion at all.

Ever since King John had signed the Magna Carta, England had a Parliament. The Members of Parliament were elected by the people, and kings were not supposed to do anything without the agreement of the Parliament. And most important was that no king could collect taxes unless Parliament agreed to it. If the King wanted extra money for some good reason, he had to ask Parliament for it.

But James had very peculiar ideas about his position as King. He even wrote a book about it — and in this book he explained that a King was more than an ordinary human being, he was chosen by God and the will of the King was at the same time the will of God. He called this "the divine right of Kings."

And as James believed in his "divine rights" he did not bother about the Parliament. Whenever he wanted money — and he needed a lot, he was a great waster of money — he told the Parliament to make taxes higher. And if the Members of Parliament refused, he ordered them to go home, closed the Parliament, and imposed higher taxes without the Parliament.

The people of England did not like that at all — no matter to which Church they belonged. So King James I of Great Britain could not be called a "popular" king, he made enemies all round.

5. Charles I

King James was an odd king; he was not cruel or evil, yet in one way or another he managed to make enemies in both his kingdoms; the Catholics called him a traitor, the Puritans and the Scots regarded him nearly as bad as the Pope in Rome, and the English people were upset by his disregard for the Parliament.

But James was never worried about the discontent amongst the people; he was so convinced of the "divine rights of kings," so convinced that, being a king, he simply could not do anything wrong — what common people thought about him just did not matter.

In ancient Egypt, it really was like this; there the people did regard the Pharaoh as a kind of divine being; but that was long ago and at the time of King James, people were no longer willing to treat kings like gods.

James simply ignored the discontent, the complaints, the bitterness amongst his subjects, and as long as he lived he did as he pleased. And when he died in 1625 he left his son a heritage of trouble.

The son, Charles, had been brought up to believe, like his father, in the "divine rights of kings;" like his father, he treated Parliament with contempt and he oppressed the Puritans.

When a kettle of water comes to the boil for a time the water simmers and bubbles — and then, quite suddenly it boils over. During the time of James the discontent of the people in Britain had been simmering, but under Charles it boiled over, and this boiling over brought civil war to Britain — British people fought and killed each other — and in the end, Charles lost his crown and his life.

The first "boiling-over" against Charles I took place in Edinburgh, in St Giles Cathedral in 1638.

Like his father, Charles wanted only one kind of Church and one kind of Church service in Great Britain: all congregations should follow the Church of England. And so he gave the order that the Prayer Book used by the Church of England had to be used in all church services in Britain.

It seems a small matter what kind of prayers people say in Church, or what words they use in a prayer. But the people of Edinburgh did not think so; they were greatly upset and angry that they were not allowed to say their prayers in their own way in Church.

When the Sunday came on which the new Prayer Book was to be used for the first time in St Giles Cathedral, there was a great crowd in St Giles, and there was much angry whispering. The Dean of St Giles entered, the congregation fell silent, and the Dean began to read from the new Prayer Book. But he had only said a few words when an old lady — her name was Jenny Geddes — shouted, "You false thief! Are you going to say Mass to my lug [ear]?" (Meaning: the new Prayer Book is like Mass in a Roman Catholic Church and you want to make me listen to it). And then Jenny Geddes, the old lady, took the stool on which she had been sitting and threw it at the minister.

In a second the whole Church was in an uproar; women pounced on the Dean and beat him with their fists; people shouted "Down with this popery!" In the end, soldiers came in and saved the Dean's life and drove the people out of the Church and into the street. But the riots continued all day long in the streets. And as the news of the riots spread, people all over Scotland, noblemen and commoners, rose in rebellion against King Charles.

The leaders of the rebellion came together at Greyfriars Church and churchyard in Edinburgh. Here they drafted a pledge that they would fight for the Church of Scotland and defend it with their lives, and many thousands of men from all over Scotland put their signatures to this pledge.

This pledge was called the "Covenant," and the men who signed it were called "Covenanters."

The Covenanters took up arms and they marched into England, where they defeated the troops King Charles sent against them. To stop further bloodshed Charles gave in and the

Covenanters returned proudly to Scotland. They had defended their right to pray and to worship the way they liked; they had revolted against their King and the King had not been able to suppress the rebellion, he had to give in and let the Covenanters have the kind of Church they wanted.

So the first rebellion against King Charles I came from the Scottish Puritans. Unfortunately, Charles did not learn his lesson from the Covenanters' rebellion; he still believed that, as a King, he had "divine rights" and that he could give orders to the English Parliament. But the English Members of Parliament were also coming to the point where their discontent also "boiled over." There were so many quarrels between King Charles and the Parliament — mostly about money and taxes — that in the end it became quite clear that King and Parliament could not rule together, either one or the other had to go.

King Charles tried to do what his father had done, but when he ordered the Members of Parliament to go home and to close the Parliament, things did "boil over." The Parliament called on the people of England to take up arms to defend their ancient rights laid down in the Magna Carta.

And King Charles called up his noblemen to fight against the rebellious commoners who dared to take up arms against their own King.

And so in 1642 the terrible Civil War in which British people fought and killed each other began.

The men who fought on the side of King Charles were mostly noblemen who rode into battle on their horses, they were called "Cavaliers" (from the French *cheval,* horse). The soldiers who fought for Parliament and its rights were called "Roundheads" because they cut their hair short, unlike the long and curled hair of the Cavaliers.

In the beginning King Charles had the better army — because the Cavaliers were men who had been trained from childhood for fighting; it was still a time when the sons of the nobility were only brought up for a career in the army, not for any other trade or profession. So, for the Cavaliers, fighting and battles were just part of life.

But the Roundheads were civilians — peasants and farmhands, shop-keepers, carpenters, tradesmen with hardly any training or experience with weapons.

And so the army of the Parliament would only have had a very poor chance of success against the Cavaliers of King Charles if they had not found a leader who knew how to make tough soldiers of men who had never drawn a sword or fired a gun before. This leader was Oliver Cromwell.

6. Cromwell and the Civil War

If we look back to early medieval times we find that the life of all people was arranged on a kind of ladder, the ladder of authority. On the lowest rung of the ladder were the villains (the feudal serfs), then came the "nobility," the knights, then came the King. Still higher up was the Church, monks, priests, abbots, bishops, and the Pope. The Pope was on the highest rung of the ladder, the highest authority of all.

But when the Age of Discovery came, when people wanted to think for themselves, the Reformation also came which meant that all over Europe people joined Churches which no longer recognized the authority of the Pope. You could say that the Protestants toppled the Pope from the top of the ladder.

But once the top authority had been thrown over, and the whole hierarchy of the Roman Catholic Church was no longer recognized, the next highest authority was the King. We have come to the time when people also turned against the King's authority; that was the next step. We saw that the Dutch turned against their lawful King, Philip of Spain, the Scots Covenanters had turned against their lawful King, Charles, and now it was the Roundheads turn to rise in rebellion against Charles in England. But you can see, it was all part of the same process: the old authorities were cast aside one by one.

The leader of the Roundheads in their fight against the Cavaliers was Oliver Cromwell. As a young man Cromwell had been the despair of his parents. They could not get him to do any useful work or study. He spent his time drinking and gambling, having drunken fights in taverns, and wasting his father's money.

But after some years of this disgraceful life, Oliver Cromwell began to get tired of all these "amusements" — they began to bore him leaving him empty and dissatisfied. Then, to everybody's surprise, he turned over a new leaf — he began to read and study, especially books about religion, and his study of these books changed him completely.

He became a Puritan of the strictest sort. He despised even the mildest forms of amusement or pleasure: his whole time was devoted to hard work, to prayer, and to reading only religious books.

As he was now such a shining example of Puritan life, it is not surprising that people were greatly impressed by this earnest and virtuous young man and they were so impressed that they elected him as Member of Parliament.

In the Parliament Cromwell soon became the foremost enemy of King Charles. He spoke again and again against the King who had no respect for the rights of the people. And so, when King and Parliament took to arms to let war decide who should rule Britain, it was only natural that Cromwell was given command of the parliamentary army, the Roundheads.

As an army-commander, Cromwell showed real genius. First of all he trained and drilled his peasants and tradesmen for endless hours every day until they were a fighting force that could hold its own with the Cavaliers. But he did more than that. He made his soldiers feel that they were fighting a "holy war" against the forces of evil, and his army life was run on Puritan rules. When his soldiers had done their arms-drill and marching, they could not simply relax — there came prayers and Bible-reading and hymn-singing. Cromwell himself was an excellent preacher and when he gave a sermon and told them that they were chosen to fight for God against sinners and servants of the Devil, the soldiers were ready to face any danger and to give their lives for the holy cause.

As a smith takes a lump of iron and forges and hammers it in the fire into a sharp sword, so Cromwell forged his army of untrained civilians into a powerful fighting force that was more than a match for the Cavaliers. At first the Cavaliers had spoken with contempt of the Roundheads but after a few battles they called them with respect the "Ironsides."

But this Civil War between the Cavaliers and Roundheads was a long war; it lasted four years, and it was a cruel and merciless war. And although it was a war between Englishmen at first, Scotland was also drawn into the fight.

The Scots Covenanters were, of course, on the side of Cromwell and they sent troops to help him. But one Scots nobleman, the Earl of Montrose; who had first been a Covenanter himself, changed his mind; he took the side of King Charles and he called upon the wild Highland Clans to come and fight for the King.

The way to raise an army in the Highlands was by doing this: a cross was made of two sticks, the ends were burnt in a fire and then dipped in goat's blood. Then this "fiery cross" as it was called was given to a clansman who ran at full speed through glens and over bens until he came to another clansman who took the cross and ran on. So the cross was passed from hand to hand until all men of that clan knew that their chief called them to war.

And so the fiery cross was sent round to call the Highland clans to the standard of Montrose, and the Highland men came in their thousands, not because they cared for King Charles but because they hated the leader of the Scots Covenanters, another Scots nobleman, the Marquis of Argyll.

Now there was Civil War in Scotland too — a war between Highlanders and Lowlanders, for the Covenanters were mostly Lowland Scots.

At first Montrose and his Highlanders were quite successful. In 1644 at Tippermuir, near Perth, the Highlanders came with a ferocious onrush upon the Covenanters — and in a few minutes the Covenanters were in full flight. Then Montrose marched on and took the city of Aberdeen. Once they had taken the city, the Highlanders robbed and plundered and killed civilians. Montrose was horrified — this was not what he wanted.

He now marched south to take Glasgow — and Glasgow surrendered without fighting. And Montrose told his Highlanders that any of them who plundered or robbed in Glasgow would be hanged. But this was not to the liking of the wild Highland men, and most of them simply left and went home. So Montrose had only a small force left, and when another army of Covenanters came against him, he was defeated. Montrose escaped from the battle and went into hiding in the Highlands — and then fled to France.

And so, in Scotland, the King's party had lost the Civil War. And soon the same happened in England.

In the battle of Naseby in 1645, Cromwell and his Ironsides defeated and completely shattered the last Cavalier army. King Charles was not there at this last battle of the Cavaliers, but when the news reached him he knew that he could not raise another army and that his cause was lost. He could not escape from England (the navy supported the Roundheads) — and soon the Roundheads would take him prisoner. In this sorry plight King Charles decided it would be better for him to be taken prisoner by Scots troops. The Scots Covenanters had sent an army to help Cromwell, and King Charles made his way to this Scottish army and surrendered himself. He asked to be taken to Scotland and to be given asylum there.

The Scots were in a quandary: they had no real quarrel with King Charles — he had given them freedom of worship and that was all they had wanted. After all Charles was the grandson of Mary Stuart, a Scots Queen — he was still King of Scotland. So the Scots decided to take Charles to Scotland. But then came a message from Cromwell, it the King was not handed over to the English there would be war between England and Scotland. Moreover the English Parliament owed the Scots two hundred thousand pounds as pay for the soldiers, and this money would not be paid to the Scots if they kept the King. Under this double threat the Scots gave in, and Charles was handed over to the English. The Civil War had come to an end.

7. The Execution of Charles

In early medieval times the "ladder" of authority existed with the serfs on the bottom rung and the Pope on the top. As we have seen, the Reformation did away with the authority of the Pope, and the next stage was that the authority of the Kings also crumbled. But this brings us to another question: which class of the people was it that turned against the ancient authorities?

In the early Middle Ages a serf who ran away from his lord and stayed in a city for a year and a day without being caught was free — he became a "citizen" who owed no obedience to any knight or lord. Freedom began in the cities, and it was first of all the city-people who followed Luther or Calvin or John Knox and became Protestants. The city-people, the "citizens" or "burghers" had this spirit of independence which, in the end, turned against the ancient authorities and toppled them from the "ladder."

The citizens or burghers were not peasants who tilled the soil, they were not knights trained for nothing but fighting, they were tradesmen — butchers, bakers, carpenters, merchants and business men. They were what we now call the "middle class."

The growth of cities during the Middle Ages had produced a new class, the citizens, or burghers or "middle class," and it was this middle class that turned first against the Pope, then against kings and at the same time against the lords and noblemen.

And the Civil War in England was really a war between the middle classes on one side and the old order, noblemen and King on the other.

You can see the clash between the old order and the new order even in the personalities of the two leaders, King Charles and Oliver Cromwell.

King Charles came from an ancient, noble family, the Stuarts who had been knights, lords, kings for many centuries. He had not *earned* the crown by great deeds or hard work, it was his by virtue of his blood, he was born with the right to become King. And Charles always showed by his proud bearing that he was fully aware of being the descendant of generations of kings.

There are pictures of Charles, showing a pale, long, aristocratic face, with long, carefully tended hair, and short, pointed beard. All the portraits show a haughty and slightly tired expression.

Oliver Cromwell was short and stumpy with a red, course face: he was by trade a beer-brewer, and he had become a leader of the Roundheads not because he was born to it but by hard work and by sheer *ability*. He had none of the graceful manners of King Charles or the Cavaliers, but he shared every hardship with his troops — he was full of fiery enthusiasm for the Puritan cause, and his soldiers loved him.

If you think of Oliver Cromwell, red-faced, stumpy, ill-dressed and ill-mannered but full of fiery energy, and of King Charles, tall, elegant, pale, proud, then you have in these two persons the whole contrast between the new class and the old class.

Now when Charles had been handed over by the Scots to the English, the English Parliament decided to keep him prisoner in a place called Holmby Hall in Northamptonshire. The Members of Parliament thought that Charles had been taught a lesson, and that, in time, it might be possible to have him as King again.

But in the meantime there came trouble between the English Parliament and Cromwell's soldiers, the Roundheads or Ironsides. The trouble was that the Parliament was short of money, and Cromwell's soldiers had not been given any pay for months. The Ironsides were quite upset about not getting paid, there was talk of mutiny and of storming the Parliament. In this situation some Members of Parliament thought the best thing would be to put Charles back on the throne, surely Cromwell and his Ironsides would not dare to go against King and Parliament together. But Cromwell forestalled this. He sent a company of soldiers to Holmby where Charles was held prisoner and these soldiers took the King away — and so he was now prisoner of his worst enemy, Cromwell.

Now Cromwell was quite determined that Charles should die – but it had to be "legal" and it had to be done with the consent of Parliament. Well, there were about 250 members of Parliament, and only a hundred of them were Puritans and on the side of Cromwell, the other 150 would rather have Charles back as King, they certainly would not have agreed to have him killed. So Cromwell sent a company of soldiers into Parliament one day, they took some members of Parliament prisoners, they drove others out — and left only the hundred (approximately) who could be relied on to do exactly what Cromwell wanted.

These remaining hundred members (called the Rump Parliament, as it was just the tail-end of the original one) now made a law that King Charles should be put before a court of law for high treason – which was quite ridiculous. The actual trial, when it came some weeks later, was utterly unfair and unjust, it was a farce. Charles was not even allowed to say anything to defend himself. The so-called judges found him guilty of high treason and condemned him to death.

When Charles was led away from the court, one soldier on guard-duty said loyally "God bless Your Majesty," an officer turned round and hit the soldier with his fist. Charles looked at the brutal officer and said: "I think the punishment was too hard for what the man did."

And on January 30, 1649 Charles was led to his death in front of a building that had once been his own palace, the palace of Whitehall in London. There was a vast crowd in the streets and some people may have wanted his death, though most of them did not, but they were all deeply impressed by the King's fearless bearing. He wanted to say a few last words to the people — but even this was denied to him for the soldiers made with their arms as much noise as they could so that no one could hear what Charles said. And so Charles knelt down and put his head on the block. When the axe had fallen the executioner in his black mask held the head up and shouted, "Behold, the head of a traitor" — but the only answer that came from the crowd was a groan.

Charles had done many foolish things in his life, but nothing wicked, he had not deserved to die like this. If anybody is to blame for the mistakes of Charles I, it is his father, James, with his ideas about the "divine rights of kings." Charles's execution did not bring peace to Britain but started a new civil war.

After the death of Charles, the Rump Parliament — the hundred odd Members of Parliament whom Cromwell had left, declared Britain a "republic" or, as they called it, a "commonwealth." But the real ruler was not this Rump Parliament, — it was Cromwell, for the Rump Parliament did only what Cromwell wanted. So Cromwell really had more power now than poor King Charles ever possessed. In our time such a man as Cromwell would be called a dictator.

The English people put up with it: they may not have liked it very much, but they put up with the dictatorship of Oliver Cromwell. The people of Scotland, however, did not.

In Scotland even the Puritans, the Covenanters, were deeply shocked when they heard King Charles had been executed like a common criminal, and they did not like a "republic" which was a republic only by name. Six days after the execution of Charles, at a meeting at the Market Cross in the High Street in Edinburgh, the Scots proclaimed the son of Charles, Charles II as their King.

Now this younger Charles, Charles II had escaped to Holland where he waited and hoped for the time when he could return and assume the crown that had been taken from his father. But young Charles made a great mistake. He thought that, as the Scots, even the Covenanters had proclaimed him King, they had forgotten the old quarrels amongst themselves, and he asked Montrose who had once led the Highlanders to raise an army in Scotland against Cromwell. Charles II himself stayed in Holland.

But the Covenanters, and their leader, Lord Argyll, had not forgotten that Montrose had quickly scattered them at the Battle of Tippermuir: they had not forgotten the robbing and murdering the Highlanders had done in Aberdeen, for which they blamed Montrose. And so they turned against Montrose when he came. They took him prisoner and he was condemned to death. Lord Argyll, the Covenanters' leader watched contentedly as Montrose was led to death. Yet, the day was not far when Lord Argyll himself would be led the same way to his own execution.

Charles II now realized that only one man could unite the Scots and rouse them to fight for him, and that was he himself. And so, in 1650, the young King (he was only twenty) landed in Scotland, and the Scots people, even the Covenanters who had rebelled against his father, now took up arms to fight for the Stuart King.

And so Britain was again thrown into civil war, a war between Scots and English.

8. England and Scotland

It is rather strange that the Scots Covenanters were willing and ready to fight for Charles II — after all they were Puritans, and had much more in common with Cromwell and his Roundheads than with Charles II, who was not a Puritan at all, but belonged to the Church of England; he was a Cavalier who liked a merry life, and did not care for the austere life of the Puritans.

So why should the Covenanters rally to the standard of King Charles? Cromwell and his Rump Parliament had executed Charles I, they had made Great Britain a "republic," a "commonwealth" without bothering to ask the Scots whether they agreed with all this or not. The Scots did not like to have rules forced on them without their consent; they had fought Charles I when he forced a new Prayer Book on them, and they were equally ready to fight against their fellow-Puritans in England who had changed the form of government — from kingdom to republic — without the consent of the Scots.

That is why the Cavalier King, Charles II, found the Puritan Covenanters of Scotland so willing and ready to fight for him.

It was Cromwell himself who led his Ironsides north and invaded Scotland to suppress the Scots' rebellion against the English Parliament.

The main fighting in this invasion of Scotland took place around Edinburgh. The Covenanters had deliberately destroyed the fields and crops in the Border-country south of Edinburgh. They had also driven off all cattle and sheep so that Cromwell's army marching through the Borders could not find any food. The English army was short of food, so Cromwell gave orders that ships laden with food should sail from England. But when the ships came they could not land, for the coast was held by the Scots Covenanters. At Berwick, at Dunbar, and at Leith there were Covenanters, and their cannons stopped the English ships from coming near.

Cromwell decided to break through to the coast and marched his hungry Ironsides towards Queensferry, but they had to pass through Corstorphine and on Corstorphine Hill there were the Covenanters, and it would have cost Cromwell half his army if he had tried to storm this hill. Imagine Cromwell standing red-faced with fury in Corstorphine, perhaps he could see his food ships in the distance on the Firth of Forth, but he could not get through to them. He had to give up his plan to get through to Queensferry; he turned his troops west and marched against Dunbar. At Dunbar the Covenanters had also strong positions on a hill, the Doonhill, which stood in the way of Cromwell's army. If the Scots had stayed on the hill, Cromwell would have had no choice but to retreat to England before his soldiers starved. But the impatient Scots made the mistake of coming down to fight the English, and in an open battle the Covenanters — who were not as well trained as Cromwell's Ironsides — were no match for these experienced soldiers. The Scots were defeated, Cromwell took Dunbar, and his ships could land and deliver food to his troops.

In the meantime Charles II tried something else to get the better of Cromwell. While Cromwell was battling at Dunbar, King Charles led another army of Covenanters south through the Borders into England. So, while Cromwell was trying to conquer Scotland, the Scots army invaded England marching south with the aim of taking London.

That was a surprise for Cromwell. What should he do? He divided his army of Ironsides into two. One half was left under the English general Monk with orders to carry on with the conquest of Scotland. Cromwell himself took the other half and hastened south to catch up with Charles II.

And Cromwell did catch up with the Scots army, at Worcester. There, on September 3, 1651, came the last grim battle of this Civil War. The Covenanters fought bravely — but again they were not as battle-hardened and experienced soldiers as the Ironsides, and at the end of the day with thousands of Covenanters dead on the battle-field, the remaining Scots troops fled in confusion. Cromwell had won the battle and the Civil War.

Charles II had escaped from the battle, but he was now a fugitive and Cromwell had promised a great reward to anyone who would capture the King. Charles had to disguise himself — he cut his long hair off and he stained his face and hands a dark brown. Fortunately for him, there were still people in England who were loyal to him and kept him hidden from the Ironsides who hunted for him everywhere.

On one occasion he was sheltered by a farmer, when the news came that a company of Ironsides was approaching. Charles climbed quickly up an oak tree. It was summer and the leaves formed a green curtain behind which he could hide. The Ironsides came riding past the tree, so near that Charles could hear them talking — but they rode by without glancing at the tree.

Later on, an English nobleman sheltered the King; Charles had to pretend he was one of the servants who looked after the horse of the nobleman's wife. But how could they get the King to the coast so that he could flee from England? The lady pretended she had to go on a journey, and Charles came with her as her servant. On the journey they had to stop at an inn, and found it full of Cromwell's soldiers.

One of them looked at Charles and said, "My friend, I think I have seen you somewhere before."

Charles answered: "That may well be so, I have travelled quite a bit with my master."

"Weren't you at one time with a Mr Baxter?" asked the soldier.

"Indeed I was," said Charles, "and you must have an excellent memory to remember me from those days. But excuse me, I must look after my lady's horse."

And so he got away from a man who never realized why that face seemed so familiar to him.

At long last Charles reached the coast on a grey, misty dawn, on a lonely stretch of the coast, a rowing boat was waiting for him and took him to a ship which brought him to France.

In the meantime poor Scotland had to pay a heavy price for having helped the King. General Monk had been left with the task of dealing with Scotland, but after the battle of Worcester and the flight of the King, the Scots had no more wish to fight on, and city after city surrendered to Monk and his Ironsides.

Now General Monk was quite determined to make these stiff-necked Scots realize that they were no longer a separate nation, and that Scotland was only a part of England.

The Scots had always had their own precious things for the coronation of a Scots king — a golden crown, a jewelled sceptre and a long sword. These three things were called the Honours of Scotland. And there was also an ancient slab of stone, the Stone of Destiny — or Stone of Scone. At the coronation the King sat on this stone when the crown was put on his head. It was said, this stone came from the Holy Land, and once upon a time Jacob had rested his head on this stone on the night when he saw in a dream God's angels moving between heaven and earth.

General Monk took this stone away from the Scots and sent it to London, and until recently it was there in Westminster Abbey. Only in 1996 was it returned to Scotland and is now in Edinburgh Castle.

General Monk had robbed Scotland of the "Stone of Scone," but he did not get the "Honours of Scotland" which he also wanted to take away. It was a minister's wife who saved them for Scotland.

9. The Lord Protector

When General Monk's army entered Edinburgh some faithful Scotsmen took the "Honours of Scotland," the crown, the sceptre, the sword from the castle and brought them to the strong fortress and castle of Dunotar. There was only a small force of Covenanters in Dunotar Castle but they were ready to fight to the last man for the "Honours." General Monk knew where the "Honours" had gone and he sent an officer and a regiment of Ironsides to get them. The Covenanters, of course, refused to surrender and the English saw no need to take the castle by storm, they surrounded the fortress and just waited until the defenders would run out of food and then would have to surrender.

Now near Dunotar there lived a Mr Granger, a minister of the Church of Scotland. Mr Granger and his wife thought of a way to save the "Honours of Scotland" before the castle would fall to the English.

One day Mrs Granger went to the officer who commanded the English troops. She asked him for permission to pass through the English lines and go up to the castle to fetch some lint which was used for bandaging wounds. There was quite a store of it in the castle and Mrs Granger said she needed some for the villagers who had run out of it.

The officer first inspected Mrs Granger's big hamper, in case she carried and food to the defenders of the castle, but the hamper was empty and so he gave her permission to go through.

Mrs Granger went up to the castle and told the defenders why she had come: to rescue the honours. At her bidding the crown and sceptre and sword were each wrapped up completely in long strips of lint and then put into the big hamper. And then heaps of lint were put on top. Mrs Granger had brought a servant with her, otherwise she would hardly have been able to carry the heavy hamper down. But between them they managed it. The English let her and the servant pass with scarcely a glance and she reached her home safely. And then, in the dead of night she and her husband buried the "Honours" in the church underneath the pulpit, and there they stayed.

A week later the defenders of the castle surrendered — but the English found no crown or sceptre and, after a long and fruitless search, had to go back to General Monk without the "Honours."

The "Honours" remained in Mr Granger's church until there was a King and crown once more, sceptre and sword were dug up and brought back to Edinburgh.

General Monk had failed to get hold of the "Honours of Scotland" — but he had Scotland in his power and he ruled over Scotland on behalf of his master, Cromwell, with an iron hand.

Cromwell himself ruled over the whole of Britain with a hand of iron. In theory, Britain was supposed to be governed by Parliament, but the Members of Parliament in Westminster were those who obeyed Cromwell's orders; they were like puppets held on strings by Cromwell.

After a time Cromwell even got tired of this Rump Parliament. One day he matched with three hundred soldiers into the Parliament and told the members: "I am going to put an end to your babbling!" And at his command the soldiers drove the dazed members out. The next day some joker put a placard on the closed doors: "House to let but unfurnished."

There was no longer anybody who could oppose Cromwell, the Cavaliers had either fled to other countries, or they had been executed. The Covenanters had been crushed, the Parliament was closed.

Cromwell was hated by the Royalists — the people who wanted Charles II back on the throne, he was hated by the Republicans who wanted Parliament to rule, he was hated by the Scots who suffered under General Monk, and hated by the English who had less freedom now that they had under Charles I.

But Cromwell had the army for himself, the Ironsides who loved him and would obey him blindly. And, moreover, Cromwell's enemies were divided and against each other — the

Scots against the English, the King's party, the Royalists, against the Republicans. And so Cromwell remained in power.

He could have made himself King — but he thought it wiser to have a King's power without using the name "King." Instead he called himself Lord Protector (as William of Orange had been "Protector" of Holland).

And as Lord Protector, Cromwell imposed the austere Puritan way of life on everybody. People were punished for getting drunk, theatres were closed, dancing was forbidden, horse-racing was forbidden, gambling was forbidden. On Sundays not even the mildest amusement was allowed: there was even a law against people "walking vainly" on a Sunday; that is, walking unnecessarily, walking for pleasure.

Cromwell had become a "tyrant" — a man who ruled without the consent of the people and who held his power only by keeping the people in fear. Anybody who spoke openly against Cromwell was in danger of imprisonment, banishment or death.

And, like all tyrants, Cromwell lived in constant fear of assassination, he feared that one of his many enemies would try to murder him. He always wore a suit of armour under his ordinary clothes — which must have been very uncomfortable. Wherever he went he was accompanied by a body-guard of Ironsides, he never dared to go for a walk by himself. And in the great palace of Westminster where he lived, he changed his bedroom every night, so that any would-be murderer would not know where to find him. So the life of the most powerful man in Britain was neither happy nor comfortable.

But in fairness to Cromwell, it must be said that he also did some good things for England. For instance, under the rule of the King the roads in Britain had never been safe for travellers; there used to be highwaymen who pounced on any wealthy-looking traveller who was lucky if they only took his money or valuables and did not murder him as well. But under Cromwell's rule the Ironsides cleared the highways, a few robbers were taken and hanged and the others disappeared.

But more important was that Cromwell made Britain a great sea-power. Under Cromwell's rule more ships were built for the British Navy than under any king. At that time three countries were trying to make themselves masters of the sea — Spain, Holland and Britain. But Cromwell made the British navy strong enough to fight and to defeat first the Spanish and then the Dutch fleets — and so it was during his time that Britain began to "rule the waves."

One result of these sea-wars was that the West Indies, the islands on the east coast of Central America, Jamaica, the Bahamas, were taken from Spain and became British colonies. These are the islands where sugar-cane is grown — and the trade in sugar and rum brought great wealth to British merchants.

But the rule of Cromwell — this uncouth countryman who had made himself the most powerful man in Britain, who was feared by the Spanish and the Dutch — this rule only lasted five years. In May 1658 Cromwell fell ill; he had worked hard, he had never spared himself and his great strength was exhausted. There came a night when a terrible thunderstorm passed over England. Thunder rolled for hours on end, lightening flashed across the sky, rain and hail fell in torrents. And in that night Cromwell, the Lord Protector, died. And a good many people in England said at that time that in this storm the Devil himself had come to take Cromwell's soul with him to hell. But this is not quite fair to Cromwell who — tyrant though he was — had never indulged in luxuries or comforts for himself and had taken his duties as a ruler more seriously than the kings before him.

When Cromwell was dying he said, "some will praise me for what I did, others will be glad of my death." Most people in Britain were glad, they were relieved that this stern ruthless man who ruled by fear was gone.

Cromwell's son, Richard, had neither the will nor the ability to rule. He abdicated — that is, he gave up the title and power of "Lord Protector" and retired to his farm in the country. So once again a Parliament was called together, once again the "republic" or "commonwealth" of Britain should be ruled by a Parliament. But things did not work out that way, for the army — the Ironsides — and Parliament did not get on together. The Ironsides, like Cromwell himself, despised the Members of

Parliament and their "blabbering" as they called it. The Ironsides had obeyed Cromwell, they were not willing to obey Parliament. So things looked pretty hopeless, for there was, really, no government at all. And at this stage General Monk, the man who had ruled Scotland on behalf of Cromwell took action to change things. He decided that the best thing for Britain would be to have again a King, to bring the King back.

You could see how often people changed sides. Monk had fought for Cromwell against the King — and now he wanted the King back.

10. The Restoration

Cromwell is a very good example of what is called a dictator; it is somebody who has come to power not because he has inherited it, like a king, and not because he has been elected like a Prime Minister, but because he took power by force. A dictator comes to power by force, and rules by force. Cromwell was the first dictator of this kind in modern history, in the history of the new age that began with new inventions and discoveries. Later on there were other such dictators — Napoleon, Hitler, Mussolini.

It is really quite strange; on the one hand we see people rise in rebellion against the old authority of the kings — but, very often, instead of freedom, there comes a new "authority" — the authority of a dictator which is worse than the old authority of the King. This is something that happens quite frequently in modern history; revolutions end in a much worst oppression.

But these dictators sooner or later die, and when they die they leave behind chaos and disorder. That was also the case when Cromwell died. Parliament and the Ironsides army were at loggerheads, there was no real government. In this situation General Monk, who had ruled Scotland for Cromwell, decided that what Britain needed was a King, and that King should be Charles II, the son of Charles I who had been executed by Cromwell.

Just think of this: General Monk had been fighting against Charles II at the time of Cromwell, he had helped in the defeat of Charles II who had to flee in disguise to save his life. And now the same General Monk wanted to bring Charles II back to the throne of Britain.

When General Monk declared himself for King Charles II he certainly had the Scots people on his side — but what about England? General Monk could not be certain about England — but he gathered an army and marched south. And as he came south he found no opposition anywhere: quite the contrary, all the way through England people cheered as Monk's army raced through. Monk led his army right into London. And in 1660 when Monk had reached London he went to Parliament and he read the Members of Parliament a message from Charles II. The message was this: If the country would receive Charles as the rightful King, he promised he would never interfere with Parliament, he would never interfere with people's religion, so that anyone could worship in his own way — he would not revenge himself on those who had fought against him, and he would not revenge his father's execution.

It was a message of generous promises — and when General Monk had read it out, all Members of Parliament cheered and they all now voted that Charles II should be restored to the throne and rule as King. This is called the Restoration.

And so Charles, who had been in France, landed at Dover and all the miles from the coast right up to his palace in London people stood in packed crowds along the roads and cheered. Nine years earlier Charles had fled in disguise, now he returned in triumph.

There was, of course, great rejoicing in Scotland. In Edinburgh the church bells were rung, trumpets sounded, cannons were fired, at night bonfires were lit. At the Mercat Cross there was a "fountain of wine" where people could drink wine like water; in the High Street there was a long table laden with cakes, sweets, fruit where everyone could help himself. Yet — if the Scots had known what was in store for them, they would not have celebrated the return of Charles II, they would have cried bitter tears.

You see, Charles had made wonderful promises — he had promised that there would be no revenge; but he had no intention to keep these promises and as soon as he was well installed, he broke every one of them.

First of all he revenged his father's death. The judges who had sentenced Charles I to death were arrested, condemned and hanged. Even the corpse of Cromwell was taken from its grave, hanged on a gallows and then beheaded.

And Charles II also broke his other promise: to allow people freedom of religion. When the Covenanters, the Scots Puritans, had fought for Charles II against Cromwell, to please the Covenanters Charles had joined their Church, the Church of Scotland. The Church of Scotland has ministers, but no bishops above them. They did not want any bishops, they thought bishops were a Roman Catholic invention. Charles had joined this Church of the Covenanters when he needed them to fight for him. But now, as King of England, he changed to the Church of England, and as King he was even head of the Church of England.

And Charles now turned against the Puritans and against the Covenanters. And like his father and his grandfather before him, he forced on the Puritans the one thing they hated the most: bishops.

You can imagine how bitterly disappointed the Scots Covenanters were, but there was one man in Scotland who thought he could persuade Charles II to keep his promises, and that was the leader of the Covenanters, the Marquis of Argyll. It was Lord Argyll who had ten years earlier put the Crown of Scotland on the head of Charles; it was Lord Argyll who had ordered the Covenanters to fight for the King, and they fought and died for him at Dunbar and Worcester. So Lord Argyll thought King Charles would be grateful to him.

But Charles had only been interested in the Scots as long as he thought they could defeat Cromwell for him. Now when he no longer needed them, he had no time for the Scots. Not once in all the twenty-five years he ruled, did he come to Scotland. And he had no time for the Covenanters, and no time for their leader, Lord Argyll. When Argyll arrived in London to see the King, he was arrested, sent as a prisoner back to Edinburgh, accused of treason against the King and condemned to death. Once Lord Argyll had watched Montrose walk to his death down the High Street of Edinburgh. Now it was his turn, as he was led to his death along the High Street.

The execution of Argyll was only the beginning of the persecution of the Covenanters. King Charles appointed a contemptible Scotsman, Lord Lauderdale, to force the Covenanters to join the Church of England. Not only did the people have to accept bishops, their own parish ministers were driven from their churches, and Lord Lauderdale put in their place ministers chosen by himself, most of them quite unfit for the task.

But the Covenanters were stubborn people; they simply did not go into churches any longer; they met in the open, on the hills and there the "outed" ministers (those who had been driven from the churches) held the services. Lord Lauderdale would not allow this either; he sent soldier to break up these meetings and to arrest any man who had taken part. But the Covenanters began to fight back.

There was the Pentland Rising when a band of Covenanters marched from the Pentland Hills on Edinburgh, but they were surrounded and defeated by the King's soldiers. Those who were killed in the fight were lucky, the others who were taken prisoners were first tortured and then hanged.

There was another battle at Bothwell Bridge on the Clyde where a whole army of Covenanters fought the King's soldiers, but the untrained Covenanters were defeated by the experienced troops. Hundreds of Covenanters died fighting, hundreds were taken prisoners and kept — ill-clad, half-starved — for months in the open in Greyfriars Churchyard, until most of them swore obedience. Those who refused were sent to America, to the West Indies, and sold as slaves to work in the sugar-plantations.

Yet in spite of the opposition — all over Scotland the Covenanters went secretly to their meetings in the glens and on the hills; they went to the meetings clutching the Bible in one hand and the sword in the other. And whenever the King's soldiers came upon such a meeting the Covenanters did not surrender but fought to the last man.

So the time of Charles II was a very unhappy period in the history of Scotland. And this was the King for whom the Scots had fought at Dunbar and Worcester, the King for whom they had saved the "Honours of Scotland."

11. The Merry Monarch

Charles II behaved shamefully in his treatment of the Covenanters; he broke his promises and he sent men who fought for him to their death. But a man like Charles just could not live in peace and friendship with the Covenanters, it was impossible, just as it is impossible for fire and ice to coexist.

Imagine what life was like in Edinburgh in the time of the Covenanters. Not only was entertainment of any kind was forbidden — but so was anything else except praying. One man was censured for visiting his sick mother on a Sunday. People were fined for wearing a new fashion — the Puritan dress was all black or dark grey. Even playing an instrument, violin or flute, was considered sinful. As you were not supposed to do any work on a Sunday you were also not supposed to do any travelling at all; if you arrived in Edinburgh on Monday you had to bring some kind of proof — a letter from the people you had stayed with — to show that you had broken your journey on Sunday and not used the Lord's day for travelling.

A true Covenanter, a true Puritan would not allow himself the smallest pleasure. In a letter of that time a Scots Covenanter wrote to a friend: "On Wednesday I planted some trees in my garden. I hope God will forgive me that I rather enjoyed doing it."

Now compare the Scots Puritan, the Covenanters, with Charles II and his courtiers. When Charles came to the throne, there came back with him the Cavaliers, and life in England changed from grim austerity of Cromwell's time to the unrestrained pleasure-seeking of the Cavaliers.

Charles and every one of his courtiers, the Cavaliers, spent literally thousands of pounds on the silk and satin of their clothes, they spent fortunes on the jewels which adorned their belts and shoe-buckles and sword-hilts and fingers. They sprayed themselves — one should better say, they soaked themselves with expensive scents and perfumes. They started a new fashion, stupid fashion, in men's hair-dos — but a fashion which was to last for more than a century — they wore wigs. Men who had perfectly good hair cut it quite short and put over it a wig with long, beautifully curled hair, down to their shoulders.

And these elegantly dressed and heavily perfumed Cavaliers devoted their time and energy whole-heartedly to amusements of any and every kind — and there was so much merry-making that Charles was called the "Merry Monarch."

The favourite occupation of the court of the Merry Monarch was gambling. They gambled with dice, they went riding and hunting, and they enjoyed a good play in a theatre just as much as a public hanging of a criminal.

And in all this pursuit of pleasure King Charles, the Merry Monarch outdid his Cavaliers, he set the example.

He was married to a Portuguese princess, but the poor Queen saw very little of her royal husband. He had chosen as his companion in all the merry-making a pretty girl he had encountered when she was selling flowers in the streets of London, her name was Nell Gwynn. Wherever the King went, it was not the Queen who was at his side, but Nell Gwynn whom and he showered with presents, money and jewels.

This was the Merry Monarch, and there could be no friend-ship and no peace between him and the Covenanters. They were as different as fire and ice.

But there is one thing one can say for the Covenanters: none of them would break a promise. On the other hand, Charles broke every promise he had given: he had taken a terrible revenge on the men who had condemned his father to death, and he did all he could to force his religion on the Covenanters.

The third promise: not to interfere with the English Parliament was not so easily broken; Charles did not want to rouse the anger of the people and cause another rebellion, another civil war. But he found another way to get what he wanted from Parliament. Many of his Cavaliers owned great estates — large tracts of land. And these great land-owners "stood for Parliament" as it is called — that is, they asked the people in their district to elect them as Members of Parliament, and the country-people voted for them. So it came that many of the Members of Parliament were Cavaliers, friends of the King, and whenever the King wanted something — money or power — they voted for him. The Members of Parliament who were elected by the country people always voted for the King's wishes.

But in the cities and towns most people were still Roundheads and so were the Members of Parliament they elected. And these Roundheads in the Parliament always voted against the King's wishes. Sometimes one party won and sometimes the other. In the old days the Cavaliers and Roundheads had fought each other with swords on the battlefields — now they fought each other with words in Parliament. And from this time onwards there have always been two parties in Parliament.

The Cavalier-party, the party of the country people, were called "Tories," the "Tory party." Of course, the party has changed very much in the course of centuries, but the Conservative Party today is still often called "Tories."

The other party, the Roundheads, the party of the cities and towns was called "Whigs." They had this name for many centuries and became the Liberal Party. Today the Labour Party still has something in common with the Roundheads, with the Puritans.

And so, when election time comes and the two great parties thunder against each other — they continue, one could say, the battles of the Cavaliers and Roundheads, but fortunately, with words and not with swords.

King Charles II had at one time — just because he needed them — joined the Puritan Church of the Covenanters; later, since it was to his advantage as King, he joined the Church of England, but when he was on his death-bed, he became a Roman Catholic. It seems that he was, in his heart, a Roman Catholic all the time.

But the next King, his brother James II, was already a Roman Catholic when he became King, and he remained one. The Stuart Kings returned to the faith of their great-grandmother, Mary Stuart, the Catholic faith.

12. The Plague and the Great Fire

Picture for a moment two ways of life: the Puritan way which Cromwell forced on England and the Cavalier way which the Restoration of Charles II brought to England. Each way of life is really an "extreme." The people who lived at that time had to go from one extreme to the other. Looking back to those times we can say: neither of these extremes is healthy; neither of these extremes is right. God would not be a loving Father if He would grudge us every joy of life, but God can also not be like one of the parents who spoil their children by granting their every wish and making life just a round of pleasures. The true way lies in the middle between the extremes.

If you look back upon Cromwell and Charles II, upon Puritan and Cavalier — they stand like a warning before you — a warning not to become like one or the other — but to find the right balance between them. So we can see history is not only something of the past, we can learn very much for this our present time from history.

Now before we go on with the history of that turbulent seventeenth century when the people of Britain were thrown from one extreme to the other, we shall look at what life was like for the common folk in those days. Although that time was only three or four hundred years ago — that's not more than ten or twelve generations ago — it was very different from our kind of life.

Just take one thing: travelling. The roads on which people had to travel were simply awful. On the main-roads the ruts made by the wheels of carts and carriages were so deep that carts often turned over. In some places there were holes filled with water and so deep that, sometimes, a horse and rider, plunging into what seemed a big puddle were almost drowned.

In Cromwell's time these roads were at least safe from highwaymen, but before and after Cromwell, no one would set out on a journey without weapons, and wealthy people were always accompanied by armed servants because the highwaymen, might take their property and life as soon as they ventured a few miles outside a town. As the only way of travelling was on horseback or in horse-drawn carriages any journey further than a few miles took endless time, was very uncomfortable and dangerous.

Fashions were colourful and elaborate — only the Puritans stuck to their plain black clothes. Remember the wigs men wore over their own hair. There is one place where this fashion of wigs for men has remained to this day: in a court of law. Judges and barristers still wear wigs when they are in court.

Now let us look at the houses. Only very rich people had brick or stone houses with many rooms and gardens. Ordinary people lived in little wattle and daub houses with wooden frames, and the space between the frames was only filled with mud or plaster. These walls kept neither the cold nor the damp out.

People were still in the habit of throwing all their rubbish out of the window into the streets — and only once in a while when the heaps of muck and dirt became so high that they blocked the street the scavengers came and carted the rubbish away.

The dirt and the stench in the streets was so awful that rich people never walked, but let themselves be carried in sedan-chairs by servants. Against the horrible smell, ladies always carried with them oranges with cloves stuck in them and held them to their noses when they passed through an especially bad stretch.

Of course, these heaps of refuse harboured countless rats. The city of London, in particular, was swarming with rats which came from the many ships in the London docks. And at the time of King Charles II some ships coming from the East brought with them a terrible contagious disease which is spread by rats (or rather by fleas living on the rats), they brought the plague.

It started in winter 1665 and, at first, only a few people here and there died and no one took much notice, nor did it occur to anybody that the rubbish heaps in the streets and the rats were a wonderful breeding-ground for the disease. But then more and more people died with the symptoms of plague (great swellings under the arm-pits) — and rich people, the King and his courtiers hurriedly left London and stayed in the clean air of the countryside.

But the common folk who had no mansions in the country-side and who had to work to earn their bread could not leave London — and they died in their thousands. As soon as one person in a house died all the other people who lived in this house were forbidden to leave it; they were not allowed to set a foot outside so that they could not spread the contagion. The doors of their house were barred from outside, and they were marked with a red cross and the words "God have mercy on us." Left to their fate, imprisoned in their own houses, whole families died of plague or starvation.

Everybody lived in dread and fear. People were afraid of each other, for your best friend, your neighbour, anybody who touched you, might infect you. When a beggar touched a man's coat the man took the coat off and threw it away, for it might have been infected with the plague.

And still people died. At one time a thousand people died every day. Whole streets became empty — there were rows of houses without a living soul in them. Only towards autumn the plague cases became fewer, and then came a very cold winter, the intense cold stopped the spread and so — after having raged for a whole year — the plague disappeared.

The city of London had not yet recovered from the ravages of the plague when, only one year later, it was struck by another terrible misfortune: the Great Fire.

Most houses in London were just wattle and daub and so would burn easily. The streets were very narrow, so that once one house was on fire not only its neighbours but also the opposite house would catch fire. If ever a city was built just right for a big fire it was London at the time of Charles II.

And the great fire came in 1666. It started at night in a baker's house, and the bakery went up in flames like a bundle of straw; the people next door in their timber houses made no attempt to stop the fire — it would have been useless. They

hurriedly collected their possessions — as much as they could
— and piled them up in the road outside, and then they watched
their homes becoming engulfed by the flames. A gust of wind
carried sparks to a nearby inn where a lot of hay was stacked up
for travellers' horses — and the hay stacks were ablaze in a
moment. By now the fire was spreading with terrific speed.
People, awakened suddenly from their sleep by the screaming
and shouting outside and the roaring flames, jumped in their
night-shirts out of their windows. The streets were packed with
men, women, children carrying bundles and pushing in all
directions.

And then the fire reached the warehouses by the river
Thames. The warehouses contained large stores of oil, of tallow
for candle-making, of hemp and of spirit. When the fire caught
these stores, they blazed till the sky was a sheet of flames.

The fire raged through the night — and the next day — and
another day — and the day after. It only came to a stop because
the wind dropped and the dock workers and other helpers had
used gunpowder to blow up houses ahead of the fire so, when
the flames came there, there was nothing to catch on.

But a very large part of London was in ashes and ruins, hundreds had lost their lives, thousands were homeless and had to
be given shelter in barns and churches in the countryside.

But, in a way, the fire was a blessing in disguise. It had
destroyed the rubbish-heaps and the rats. And London was
rebuilt and was built according to a plan and not higgledy-pig-
gledy as it had been. But the Great Fire is still remembered in
the round "London's burning."

The reign of the Merry Monarch was not a happy time for
the people of London who suffered two catastrophes, two great
misfortunes at the time of Charles II.

13. The Glorious Revolution

When Charles II died in 1685, his brother, James became King though he was a Catholic. It is rather surprising that the English Parliament, where all members were Protestants should agree to have a Roman Catholic as King. But both parties, Tories and Whigs, would rather have a rightful King — which James II was — than plunge the country into another civil war. James had to give a promise not to interfere with the Protestant Churches, and as long as he kept this promise the English Parliament was willing to have him as King.

But it was different in Scotland, the Scots Covenanters said: "Under the law of Scotland a Catholic cannot be King of Scotland. We have no king, James is *not* our king." And this stubborn refusal to recognize James as the rightful King brought great suffering to Scotland — for James decided to make an end of these rebellious, disobedient Covenanters. The man he appointed to deal with the Covenanters was Lord Claverhouse, a man who was as ruthless and merciless as the Duke of Alba had been. Claverhouse sent his soldiers to hunt down the Covenanters as they had never been hunted before.

The Covenanters still had their forbidden prayer-meetings in the hills — but any who were caught at it were executed — or if they were lucky they had one ear cut off and were then sent as slaves to America and sold like cattle.

The worst example of the fury of Claverhouse and his men are the Wigtown Martyrs. In Wigtown the soldiers of Claverhouse arrested two women — one sixty years old, the other only twenty — named Margaret Lauchleson and Margaret Wilson. The two women were asked if they were willing to join the Church of England. When they refused they were taken to the seashore and tied to stakes at low tide, and when the tide rose they were drowned.

The time of King James II, the time of his henchman, the

cruel Claverhouse is the worst, the most terrible time in the whole history of Scotland. Yet, James was himself of Scots descent, a Stuart, the great-grandson of Mary Stuart.

But it was not only the Scots Puritans, the Covenanters who refused to have a Roman Catholic as King: there were also English Puritans who were against James, and there were Scots and English Puritans who had fled from Britain to Holland and who planned and prepared a rebellion against James.

The leader of the Scots Puritans in Holland was Lord Argyll — the son of Lord Argyll who had been put to death by Charles II. Argyll landed in Scotland, hoping to rouse the whole country against the King and against Claverhouse. But, as it happens so often in Scots history, they bickered and quarrelled, and nothing came of the rebellion. Argyll was caught by the King's soldiers and executed in Edinburgh, like his father.

The English leader of the Puritan rebellion, Monmouth, fared no better. He landed in England and thousands of men joined him, but they were defeated in battle and Monmouth was captured and executed. The Puritan rebellion against James failed in England as well as in Scotland.

But what the rebellious Puritans had always said — that a Roman Catholic king would try to bring the Church of Rome back — was really true. For James, in spite of the promise he had given, did plan once again to make Britain a Catholic country.

He certainly did everything to favour Roman Catholics; in the army Protestant officers were dismissed and Catholics put in their place, at Oxford University Protestant teachers were sent away and Catholics put in their place.

The English Parliament had stood faithfully and loyally by James against the rebels, Argyll and Monmouth, but neither of the two parties liked what was going on afterwards. They began to think that James had to go. But who should take his place?

James had a daughter, Mary, who had married a Dutch nobleman, William of Orange, the great-grandson of the William who had fought the Spaniards. This William of Orange was a Protestant and the English Parliament began to think they would rather have a king who was Dutch but a Protestant, than James who was British but Roman Catholic.

And then James did something which really infuriated Parliament and all the people in England and Scotland. He passed a law without asking first for the agreement of Parliament. The law itself was really only fair — the Roman Catholic Church should have the same rights as any other Church — but what upset the people of Britain and Parliament was that the King made laws without Parliament; he had no right to do so. It also confirmed their fears that James was trying to make the country Roman Catholic.

So Parliament sent a message to William of Orange to come and drive James out and to take his place as King.

In November 1688, William had a fleet ready to invade England. On the ships were large flags with the inscription "I will maintain the liberties of Britain and the Protestant religion." The fleet landed in Devon and an army of fifteen thousand went ashore, the largest army to invade Britain since Roman times.

But the army of William of Orange was not an army of conquerors — where they marched people came out to welcome the troops and cheered.

James himself led an English army against the invaders, but his own soldiers, his own generals deserted him and went over to join William of Orange. There was no fighting and no battle, for James had no soldiers left who would fight for him.

James was captured. However, William had no wish to execute the father of his wife, his father-in-law. James was allowed to flee to France. He never saw Britain again.

The wonderful thing about this revolution against James was that it took place without any bloodshed at all and therefore in all history books it is called the Glorious Revolution. The year of the Glorious Revolution is 1688, exactly a hundred years after the Great Armada.

Both England and Scotland were jubilant and gladly accepted William as King. In fact he and his wife, Mary, were to rule together, so this is called the reign of William and Mary.

The Scots Covenanters were of course jubilant, now they could have their own ministers and worship in their own churches without fear of persecution.

But the cruel Claverhouse fled to the Highlands. Many of the Highland clans were still Roman Catholics; they sheltered Claverhouse and he even persuaded them to rise in rebellion against William.

And so once again, Scotsmen fought each other, the Lowlanders for William and the Highlanders against the new King. But in this battle of Killiecrankie in 1689, Claverhouse was killed and although the Highlanders won the battle, they gave up and did not go on with the rebellion.

To make certain that from now on the Highland clans would keep the peace a fort was built at the foot of Ben Nevis. It was called Fort William, in honour of the new King, William of Orange. Although it is no longer a fortress, the place is still called Fort William today. Fort William still reminds us of the "Glorious Revolution" of 1688 which brought William and Mary to the throne.

14. The Union of 1707

All the Stuart Kings (James VI, Charles I, Charles II, James II) had been clinging to the belief that a king had "divine rights," rights which God had given to him. But William of Orange could not claim "divine rights" — he had been put on the throne by the Parliament and had only such rights as Parliament gave him. From William onwards no king or queen ever went against the wishes of Parliament, and as time passed the kings had less and less to say. In the end it was the Parliament which ruled the country, not the kings and queens.

And the Parliament is only the assembly, the gathering of the men and women who are elected as Members of Parliament by the rest of the population. And the population can change their minds every five years when there are new elections and can change the government.

At first the Scots had their own Parliament; it was in Edinburgh, in the building now called the Law Courts behind St Giles Cathedral. The Scots made their own laws there and the English made their own laws in London. But after a time the leaders of the Scots Parliament agreed that it would make the work of government simpler if the Scots Members of Parliament would sit together with the English Members of Parliament in London. And so the Scots Parliament in Edinburgh was closed — and the Scots and English had the one Parliament in London together. This was the "Union" in the year 1707.

The Scots Members of Parliament had agreed that this was the best for the complicated job of governing Britain, but the common people in Scotland did not like it at all. They had been proud of their own Parliament. There were riots in Edinburgh, and even worse riots in Glasgow. Later on people quietened down — but there was a good deal of anger and discontent in Scotland.

Now there were people who were very pleased that there was trouble in Scotland. When James II had to flee from England, he did not give up his throne willingly. He was convinced that he was the rightful King, a King by the "Grace of God" and Parliament had no right to drive him out. He continued to call himself King and never gave up the hope that either he himself or his son would one day return to the throne of Britain.

And there were also people in Britain, specially amongst the Highland Clans of Scotland, who thought that James was the rightful King and who wanted him or his son to return as ruler of Britain. The people who were for King James were called "Jacobites" (James in Latin is Jacobus).

There were Jacobites in Scotland, there were some in England and there were some who had followed James and stayed with him in France. And when James II died, the Jacobites in France proclaimed his son, also called James, as the new rightful King of Great Britain. He was called the "Pretender" — for he had pretensions to be King.

The Jacobites and their Pretender were very pleased to hear of the trouble in Scotland — to hear that many Scots people disliked the Union and were angry about it. The Jacobites thought that if they started a rebellion in Scotland they would get many supporters: they only waited for the right moment. And this right moment came — or at least the Jacobites thought so.

When William and Mary died in 1702, their daughter Anne became Queen, but Anne never married and when she died in 1714 there was no successor to the throne. But there was a distant relative in Germany — he was the grandson of a daughter of James VI (James I of Great Britain) — who was the ruler of a tiny province in Germany, called Hanover. This distant relation, George of Hanover, was the man who was chosen by the British Parliament to become King of the United Kingdom.

All the kings and queens who have ruled since, including Queen Elizabeth II, are descendants of this German prince, George of Hanover.

Now George had really very little to recommend him as King of England and Scotland — except that he was a Protestant and that he was distantly related to James and Mary Stuart. But otherwise there was little to recommend him. He could not speak a word of English and as he was already fifty-five years old when he was called to England, it was too late for him to start learning. In any case, he did not even bother to try.

In one way, it did not matter — it was the Parliament which ruled the country, not the King. But, on the other hand, the people of England and Scotland could hardly be very fond of a King who could not talk to them in their own language. That is why the Jacobites and their Pretender thought that the coming of George I was the right moment to start a rebellion.

The Pretender came secretly over to Scotland, and at the house of a Jacobite nobleman, the Earl of Mar, the Highland Chiefs gathered to meet him and pledge their support. And so began the first Jacobite rebellion in 1715 — and it ended in disaster. The rebels were beaten by the government troops in the battle of Sheriffmuir, many Highlanders lost their lives and the Pretender and his friend Mar escaped to France.

But the failure of the 1715 rebellion did not discourage the Jacobites. They now planned to have another rebellion when Britain would be at war with another country and so would have no troops to spare for fighting rebels. But they had to wait for this chance. When it came it was not the Pretender, but his son, Charles Edward — or as he is called Bonnie Prince Charlie, who led the rebellion.

Bonnie Prince Charlie was a good-looking young man, fair-haired, dark eyed, elegant, witty and brave. Moreover he had the charm of his grand-uncle Charles II and so could gain the friendship of men and the love of women easily.

But this charming young man was also ambitious and determined to win back the throne which his grandfather had lost, and the people who should help him to win the crown should be the Scots.

If you think how much the Scots suffered under the Stuart Kings — under Charles I, Charles II, James II — it is strange that he should count on the Scots to help a Stuart. But first of all, it had been the Lowlanders, the Covenanters, who had suffered most — not the Highlanders. And Prince Charles Edward also counted on the fact that many Scots would sooner have a Scots family, the Stuarts on the throne, than a German family, the Hanoverians.

When war broke out between Britain and France, the Jacobites seized the chance they had been waiting for, and Bonnie Prince Charlie — as his father had done — came secretly to Scotland to start a rebellion. Once again Scotland was to become a battlefield.

15. The Jacobite Rebellion

It was natural that Bonnie Prince Charlie should first turn to the Scots Highlanders for help. Many Highlanders were still Roman Catholics like himself, and they also loved fighting; they had followed Montrose against the Covenanters, they had followed Claverhouse against William of Orange, they had followed the Pretender against the government army. That is why Bonnie Prince Charlie landed in 1745 at Eriskay in the Outer Hebrides and sent messages to the Highland Chiefs to come and fight for him. The Chiefs were at first not very willing — they remembered too well how badly things had gone for them in the 1715 Rising. But when Bonnie Prince Charlie said to Lochiel, Chief of the Cameron Clan, "Will you sit at home and read about my battles in newspapers?" the chief felt ashamed and said, "No, I and my clan will be with you." And the other chiefs also pledged their clans to fight for the Prince.

So Bonnie Prince Charlie raised his standard of red silk at Glenfinnan and the Clansmen — summoned by the fiery cross — gathered. They put a "cockade" (a white rosette) on their bonnets, for that was the Stuart emblem.

One month after his arrival in Scotland, the Prince had an army of three thousand fierce Highlanders and as he led this army into the Lowlands, other volunteers joined him so that his army grew as it marched along.

His first objective was the city of Edinburgh — and with the exception of the Castle, Edinburgh surrendered without fighting. The castle was held by regular soldiers of King George II who held out and did not surrender.

But this did not worry Prince Charlie. He rode into Edinburgh and there were great crowds to welcome him. There were even people trying to touch his clothes as he rode past, or to kiss his hands.

There were also Edinburgh people who did not join the

cheering, they had not forgotten the cruelties of Claverhouse and the Wigtown Martyrs; but most of the womenfolk of Edinburgh were enchanted by this good-looking young man, he seemed to them like a prince from a fairy-tale.

That night he gave a great party at Holyrood Palace, there was music and dancing and laughter in the old palace which had not seen such a merry gathering since the days of Mary Stuart.

In the meantime, however, the Government in London had not been idle. Orders and messages had gone out and an English army was coming up from Dunbar. And in the early morning after the great party Prince Charles (who could only have had little rest) led his troops out of Edinburgh to meet the enemy. Armies moved slowly in those days and it took them the whole day to cover the nine miles (15 km) to Prestonpans where they came face to face with the English. As it was so late, neither army went into battle, the soldiers lay down in the fields for a night's sleep. But in the darkness a local man who knew every inch of this part came and showed the soldiers of Charles a narrow path through a bog which took them behind the Government troops and to surprise them with an attack from an unexpected quarter. When daylight came and Prince Charles gave the signal to attack, the English troops were, indeed, taken by surprise; they were in such utter confusion that the whole battle was over in a short time. The foot soldiers were all captured or killed, only the horsemen escaped by riding away as fast as they could. After this splendid victory Prince Charles returned to Edinburgh where he spent a whole month in royal splendour.

By then a good many Edinburgh people were a bit less happy about the visit. They had always regarded the Highlanders as savages and they were not too pleased to see these "wild men of the hills," with their uncivilized habits amongst the more refined citizens of Edinburgh.

But after a month of pleasure and feasting Prince Charles left Edinburgh and led his army south into England. The cities and towns on his way all surrendered without fighting — and it seemed that nothing could stop him. But the Highlanders became tired of marching and marching: and the further they got away from Scotland the more despondent they became. First a few, and then more and more simply deserted, running away and making their own way back to their homes.

Prince Charles had no choice but to turn back, or his whole army would have melted away like snow in the sun. The soldiers were happy marching back, but they did not know that they had thrown away Bonnie Prince Charlie's chance to win the crown of Britain, for King George in London had already been packing to flee to Germany.

And while they marched back, the Government in London had time to gather new armies to fight against the Prince. Yet, Prince Charles was once more victorious at Falkirk. But this victory did not help him at all because the Highlanders refused to stay in the Lowlands, and Charles had to march them to Inverness. The Prince was furious — he was so angry that he dashed his head against a wall in a fit of temper — but he had to go to Inverness. And even there the Highlanders began to desert him. When at long last an English army came, Prince Charles had only half the number of men the English had. In the battle which followed at Culloden Moor, the remaining Highlanders fought with the old Highland courage and bravery, but they were up against trained and experienced soldiers. The English were in three lines: the front-line kneeling, the second row stooping, the third standing, and all three lines with rifles at the ready. And every time the Highlanders charged they were mown down by the rifle-fire. The day ended with the utter defeat of Bonnie Prince Charlie. The battle of Culloden Moor in 1746 was the last time British people fought each other in civil war.

Charles fled and for five months he was kept hidden in the Highlands. A prize of £30,000 was offered for him by the Government, but none of the poor Highland crofters who sheltered the Prince ever betrayed him.

The person who helped him most was a beautiful Highland lady, Flora MacDonald. At one time she brought him a woman's dress and he went about as Flora's maid, Betty. Flora MacDonald risked her life for the Prince by helping him but she did it willingly. It was a sad day when at long last, it was possible to get Bonnie Prince Charlie on a boat, it was a sad day for her when he said good-bye to her — and they never saw each other again. He escaped to France and spent the rest of his life travelling about; he died forty-two years later in 1788, a broken, unhappy man in Rome.

But the Highlanders paid a terrible price for their rebellion. Hundreds were tortured and executed, their homes destroyed, their families left to starve. The Highland dress, kilt and tartan, was forbidden, so were their songs and the bagpipes. Even the use of the Gaelic language was forbidden. A man would be sold as a slave to America for even possessing a kilt.

Many Highlanders and also Jacobites from the Lowlands fled — but they could never return to their homelands, and they spent their lives in foreign lands always longing for hills and glens they could never see again.

After the battle of Culloden Moor the old Scotland died, and the new Scotland that later emerged had to face a modern world where people had other things to worry about than the claims of the Stuart Kings, or what kind of Prayer Book is used in Church.

16. Past and Future: Russia and Germany

The Stuarts' time — from James VI to Bonnie Prince Charlie — was a time of upheaval, unrest and civil war in which the people of Britain fought each other, royalists and republicans, Puritans and Cavaliers, Scots and English, Catholics and Protestants. The Stuarts were basically trying to preserve the old order — the divine rights of kings, and ultimately even the Church of Rome. The Stuarts, in one way or another, tried to defend the old system of authority, and all the battles and wars and rebellions were really a long drawn out conflict between those who fought for the past and those who fought for the future.

But this great conflict between forces of the past and forces of the future was not only taking place in Britain, but took place all over Europe. In Britain it was the Kings, the Stuart Kings who stood for the past, and Cromwell and the Puritans — the Roundheads — who fought for the future, but in Russia it was just the opposite.

In Britain, in the West of Europe, the kings stood for the past, and the common people wanted to change things. King James and all the other Stuarts wanted to prevent any change — things should stay as they had been for centuries. The common people had to fight for the changes which had to come.

In the East, in Russia, the strange thing was that a ruler, an emperor, forced his people, much against their will, to accept changes and to take part in the modern world which was coming. It was just the opposite here: the changes came from the emperor, not from the people.

After Genghis Khan, the Tartar warrior, had conquered China and then Russia, for centuries Russia remained under the rule of the Tartars who treated the Russians like slaves. Eventually after a long time, the Tartars were driven out, and the Russians had their own rulers called "tsars" (which comes from "Caesar"). But the Russian people had been enslaved for so long that, even when the Tartars were no longer their masters, they were not used to anything else and remained slaves of their new masters, the tsars. The tsar of Russia was not like any other king in Europe — he really had "divine rights," he had absolute power over the life of every Russian. One of these rulers of Russia, Ivan the Terrible, who lived at the time of Queen Elizabeth, had hundreds of thousands of Russians executed for no good reason at all. Most people accepted that the tsar had the right to kill as many of his subjects as he liked. It is no wonder that Russia was the most undeveloped country in Europe, even noblemen were illiterate, the peasants were feudal subjects who could not determine their own life, and few inventions and discoveries from western Europe had penetrated Russia.

But at the time when Britain was ruled by the Merry Monarch, Charles II, there came a tsar in Russia who brought great changes: Peter the Great who ruled from 1689 to 1725. Peter travelled outside Russia, accompanied by courtiers and noblemen, to study the knowledge of the western countries in order to bring it back to Russia. He wanted to learn how to build great ships, how to build roads, how to train soldiers; he was interested in everything. When he came to London for the first time he saw a dentist at work — and he was so enthusiastic about this man's skill, that he himself practised pulling teeth on his unfortunate courtiers.

When he returned to Russia he brought with him five hundred English and Scots experts, mechanics, ship-builders, surgeons, architects, and a Scotsman (Peter Gordon) was given the task of training the wild, undisciplined Russian soldiers. From Holland Peter took with him clock-makers and book-printers, and so he returned to Russia with an army of foreigners who were to change life in Russia from top to bottom.

But the Russians did not want any changes, they did not want better houses or ships or cities, they did not want doctors and schools. Some of Peter's own noblemen and courtiers plotted to murder the tsar who was trying to change the old Russian way of life, and Peter's own son, Alex, took part in this plot. But the conspiracy was betrayed and all who had taken part in it were executed. Alex died in prison, otherwise he would have been beheaded like the others. Peter was a ruthless man: Russia was to become a modern nation and anybody who stood in the way was his enemy and had to die.

He was equally ruthless when he wanted to build a new city, St Petersburg on the Baltic coast. A hundred and fifty thousand peasants were driven by soldiers to the site of the city, and as there were not enough spades, they had to dig with their bare hands. There were not enough carts, so the peasants had to carry bricks and earth in their hands. Thousands of workers died of hunger or of cold, but in ten months the city was built.

Peter the Great forced the Russians, against their will, to become a modern nation. He had the "divine rights of kings" — which the Stuarts only wanted but never had. But Peter used his "divine rights" for *progress,* for changes — while the Stuarts tried to *prevent* changes. In the West, in Britain, the people fought against the monarch to get things changed, in the East, in Russia, the monarch, Tsar Peter, forced the people to accept changes. And what about the middle of Europe, Germany and Austria? In Germany the upheaval was far worse than either in the West or in the East.

Germany and Austria were supposed to be ruled by an emperor, but in fact, the emperor had very little power. Each German lord or prince ruled his own little part of Germany as he pleased and took little notice of the emperor. All the Protestant noblemen banded together in one great union, all the Catholic noblemen formed another union, and they started a war that lasted for thirty years. The emperor, Ferdinand II, was himself a Catholic and the leader of the Catholic league.

For thirty years, 1618–48, armies marched across Germany, fought battles, destroyed cities, devastated fields, robbed and plundered. Other countries got mixed up in the war: the King of Sweden came with an army to help the Protestants, the French sent troops to help the Catholics, but it only brought more suffering to the people of Germany. Whole provinces which had been flourishing, became deserts; prosperous towns became ruins.

The Thirty Years' War, as it is called, only came to an end because both sides were too exhausted to carry on. When peace was made the Protestants and Catholics were still not willing to live in peace together, but they agreed that if the prince or lord who ruled a province of Germany was a Protestant, then all the people under him should be Protestants, and the Catholics had to leave this province and go to a part of Germany ruled by a Catholic Prince who had driven out the Protestants under his rule. And so Northern Germany became mainly Protestant and Southern Germany, Bavaria, and Austria became mainly Catholic.

The whole of Germany had suffered so much, and so much had been destroyed that it took a century until Germany had recovered from the ravages of the Thirty Years' War.

The seventeenth century which saw the Civil War in England and Scotland, also saw great upheavals in other parts of Europe: the Thirty Years' War in Germany, and the changes which Peter the Great brought to Russia.

The French Revolution

17. The Huguenots

At the time when Leonardo da Vinci experimented with flying machines, and when Columbus and Magellan sailed out into unknown seas, and when Copernicus dared to say that contrary to what everybody could tell, the earth revolves around the sun, not the sun round the earth, at that time — around the fifteenth century — there began a new age for mankind, it was like a great awakening. And with this great awakening there came a new sense of freedom.

People would no longer blindly accept the authority of the Pope in Rome, and this rebellion against the authority of the Church led to the Reformation. Luther in Germany, Calvin in Switzerland and John Knox in Scotland found thousands of followers and became the founders of Churches which no longer regarded the Pope in Rome as the supreme authority and master.

But in addition, this rebellion against the authority of the Pope soon became a rebellion against kings. The Dutch rose against their ruler, King Philip II of Spain and gained their freedom. And in Britain, too people would no longer regard a king as someone who has "divine rights." Charles I paid with his life for trying to rule by "divine right," and although Charles II, the Merry Monarch, came to the throne, his successor and brother, James II, lost it again in the Glorious Revolution of 1688. The people of Britain did not want kings who claimed they had divine rights — that time was past, and so, Bonnie Prince Charlie's attempt to regain the crown of Britain for the Stuarts was really doomed from the start. The new age, the newly awakened minds of the people would no longer put up with kings who believed in their divine right to rule.

But, whenever and wherever something new comes into the world, there are more than the people who welcome the new with heart and mind, there are also the people who hate what is new, and want to stop human progress.

The Popes in Rome were certainly not pleased with the rebellion against their authority. They would have put Luther before the Inquisition and they would have burnt him at the stake, if Luther had not had such a great number of followers in Germany. In Germany the Popes did not have enough power to harm Luther, but in Italy the Popes had the power to fight the new spirit. They burnt the monk Savonarola in Florence who had dared to call the evil Pope Alexander Borgia "a son of the devil." They burnt another monk, Giordano Bruno, because he had dared to say the earth was a planet in the cosmos and revolved around the sun. And Galileo Galilei escaped torture and death only by denying the truth about the earth in which he believed: that the earth moves around the sun.

In Italy the new spirit, the spirit of the Reformation, the spirit of discovery and science was suppressed. In Spain the Popes found willing helpers in the kings — remember how Philip of Spain tried to win Holland and England by force for the Church of Rome, but failed miserably.

And now we come to another European country where the kings also tried with all their might and power to stop the march of progress, to turn the clock back, and to rule by "divine right." And they succeeded for a time — for quite a long time, two hundred years. But, in the end, the last of these kings paid a terrible price for the mistakes made by the kings who had ruled before. The country where this happened was France.

France, the land of Charlemagne, the land of Joan of Arc, had for many centuries been a land that was devoutly Roman Catholic, and obedient to the Pope. The Knights of France were the first knights who followed the Pope's call for a Crusade against the Turks. And it was also in France that the first and more beautiful Gothic churches with pointed arches and stained-glass windows had been built.

But France was also the country where the feudal system was harsher and lasted longer than in most other countries. In France for a very long time the peasants remained serfs who could be bought and sold with the land like the trees that grew on it. And in France, too, the knights and noblemen were under strict obedience to the king. In France there was no Magna

Carta, which set out what a king was and was not allowed to do. In France the will of the King was the law, and the King had only one master above him: the Pope in Rome. That's how it was in France, and that's how the kings of that country wanted it to stay forever.

And then came the time of the Reformation. John Calvin who was a Frenchman had to flee from France to Switzerland. But from Geneva his teaching spread to France, and many thousands of Frenchmen became Protestants, or, as they were called in France, Huguenots. There were so many of these Huguenots, even amongst the noblemen and lords, that it seemed as if the King of France, whether he liked it or not, could do nothing about it. In fact, it seemed that in France Protestants and Catholics would live in peace together. But it only seemed so. The King at that time (Charles IX) was a weak person who left the government entirely in the hands of his mother, an Italian Princess, Catherine de Medici.

Catherine de Medici was quite determined to destroy the French Protestants, the Huguenots, but not by an open attack. This cunning queen knew that if it came to an open, armed conflict between Catholics and Protestants, it might take years and the whole country would be ruined by civil war until the Protestants were suppressed. Instead of this, Catherine de Medici and her advisers, planned to destroy the Huguenots with one blow that should come down on them without warning.

In great secrecy all the Roman Catholics were informed that on the day of St Bartholomew, August 24, at night, all people known to be Huguenots were to be wiped out, and it was the duty of every good Catholic to do his share of the killing. And — strangely enough — the secret was kept; the Protestants heard no whisper and went peacefully about their business and talked with their Catholic neighbours without any idea what was planned for them.

A few days before chalk-marks were made on the houses where Huguenots lived, but the Huguenots hardly noticed these marks and gave no thought to them.

The day of St Bartholomew, August 24, 1572, passed quietly, but when darkness fell a signal from the Royal Palace in Paris was given, and parties of armed soldiers started the horrors of this night. They stormed into the houses marked with chalk and killed every man, woman and child they found. And once the soldiers had started the massacre, the Roman Catholic citizens armed themselves and joined in and fell on their unsuspecting Protestant neighbours. It was one of the worst massacres in history.

Most of the killing took place in Paris where many Huguenots lived. But there were also other parts of France where these horrible murders took place. Altogether, thirty thousand Protestants were killed in this one night. The event is called the Massacre of St Bartholomew's Night.

A few thousand Huguenots escaped to England where they were well received and helped. Many of these Huguenot refugees brought new skills to Britain and so repaid the kindness shown to them.

But, in France, Catherine de Medici, had achieved what she wanted. By wiping out the Protestants, she had not only earned the gratitude of the Pope, she had also made sure that for a long time to come, that people in France would not dare to challenge the authority of either Pope or King. The Massacre of St Bartholomew's Night had kept the new spirit out of France — at least for a time.

18. *Le Roi Soleil*

Catherine de Medici was certainly an evil woman; one can hardly imagine the kind of soul who planned and quite calmly arranged the massacre of thousands of innocent people. But, on the other hand, in the time in which Catherine lived, the killing of people who had a different faith was quite common. In Britain while the Protestants killed each other — Church of England against Covenanters — Catherine was only more cunning in her ways, but otherwise she only did what was being done all over Europe in the terrible century that followed the Reformation.

Imagine that Catherine were brought before a court of law for the massacre of St Bartholomew's Night; she could have said in her defence: "By this one night of bloodshed I saved France from years of civil war in which far more than thirty thousand would have been killed. Look at the Thirty Years' War in Germany, look at the Civil War between Roundheads and Cavaliers in Britain. In Germany and in Britain far more lives were lost, far more suffering was caused than the deaths and suffering of that one night in France. Moreover I saved the power of the kings in France. In Britain the Stuart Kings lost their power, in Germany the Emperor had to give in to his noblemen and lords. Only in France the power of the King not only remained, but grew even stronger."

Of course, in reality Catherine could not have spoken like that, for the Thirty Years' War in Germany, the Civil War in Britain, came years after her death. But she could and did realize that the old order, the old authority of King and Pope would be overthrown, civil wars would rage — and the Massacre of St Bartholomew's Night was her way to prevent this from happening.

And so, in the following century, while in Britain the power of kings crumbled and was swept away, in France the power of the King grew stronger, it became *absolute power,* as it is called.

And while Britain and Germany were shaken by civil wars France prospered. While in Britain, King James wrote books and talked about the "divine rights of kings," and James's son, Charles I, lost his life in trying to rule by "divine right," at the same time in France there was a King who indeed ruled by "divine right" — who ruled with absolute power. This king was Louis XIV.

There was a kind of parliament in France, it was called the "Estates General," but these Estates General could only advise the King, they could *ask* him to do this or that, they could ask him *not* to do this or that, but they could not interfere with anything he wanted to do. Nothing can illustrate the whole situation better than the words spoken by Louis XIV on one occasion.

It happened eleven years after Charles I had been beheaded in front of his palace in Britain. At that time, in 1660, Louis XIV, King of France was only twenty-two years old. However, he already had very expensive tastes — he wanted to build an enormous new palace for himself. There was not enough money in the treasury and so he sent a command to his parliament — to the Estates General — to increase the taxes.

Having sent a messenger with this request to the assembly, Louis went hunting, a sport in which he took great pleasure. When he came back from the hunt he was told that the noblemen of the Estates General were very unhappy about his demand for making the taxes higher, they thought the taxes paid by the French people were already too high and it would mean great hardship to make them still higher. Young King Louis was furious. He rode in his hunting outfit, as he was, to Paris and to the building where the assembly had gathered. With his riding-whip in his hand he entered and strode into the great hall.

All the members of the Estates General stood up as His Majesty, a youngster of twenty-two, walked in. Louis looked at them contemptuously and said, "What is all this nonsense about the taxes? I need the money."

One of the members replied, "Most Gracious Majesty, forgive us for speaking freely but we all here are in agreement that it is not good for the state if so much money is to be spent on a new palace, the state cannot afford to waste money on such unnecessary luxuries, we must consider the state of France as a whole, we must have a regard for the state first and then ..."

"The state, the state," shouted Louis furiously, and he hit a desk before him with his riding-whip. "The state, *L'état, c'est moi* [I am the state]." And with these words he turned his back and walked out. And the assembly could do nothing else but obey and make taxes higher.

These words, *"L'état, c'est moi"* have become famous in history, for they give a picture of how a King of France thought of himself. He thought of himself as a kind of sun which spreads light everywhere. If somebody speaks of light, the sun could say: "What are you talking about: I am the light, I am the source of light." And, in the same way, Louis XIV thought of himself: "I am France, I am the state of France, and my glory is the glory of France." And naturally expected his courtiers to call him *le Roi Soleil,* the "Sun-King."

As far as Louis XIV was concerned, everything that was done in the whole of France had only one purpose: to glorify himself, the King of France. The peasants who worked in the fields, the tradesmen who worked in the cities, the merchants who did business, they all had one duty and one purpose alone: to provide the monarch with the money he needed and with the luxuries such a king must have.

The painters, the sculptors, the architects had only one duty, one purpose: to surround His Majesty, Louis XIV, with beauty and to glorify the greatness of the King in pictures, statues and buildings.

The noblemen, knights and lords of France had only one duty, one purpose in life: to surround the King, amuse and entertain him, serve him on hand and foot and enjoy the great privilege only granted to men and women of noble birth: to be in the presence on the *Roi Soleil,* the Sun-King. Similarly the soldiers of France only had one duty and one purpose: to fight for the *Roi Soleil,* to make new conquests for him and, by these conquests, bring greater glory to the King of France.

For the sake of this glory through conquests, Louis XIV plunged France into one war after another. In 1667 his armies invaded Holland — for no reason other than the King's glory. But the Dutch called a powerful ally to their aid: the sea. They opened dikes and though the floods ruined the land for years, they saved Holland from being conquered by France.

Another war which Louis XIV started was the War of Succession. It was a war for the crown of Spain. The King of Spain had died without children — and Louis XIV claimed the throne of Spain for himself.

Now if Spain and France had become one country it would not only have been the most powerful in Europe but it would also have ruled the great Spanish colonies in South America, and the great colony of Canada which was at that time belonged to France. It would have been an empire of enormous power — and Britain and Germany were afraid that, sooner or later, Louis with his mad ambition, would conquer them too. So Britain and Germany joined forces and fought against Louis to prevent him from becoming ruler of France and Spain.

This was the "War of Succession" that lasted for ten years. This war raged not only in Europe, but also in America. In America too the English colonists and the French colonists fought against each other.

If this was not enough, Louis XIV, who called himself the "most Christian King" called the Muslims Turks to his aid. In 1683 the Turks came over the Balkan peninsula and invaded Austria and laid siege to Vienna. But Vienna held out, and the Turks were driven back.

In the end France lost. The British took a large part of Canada (although not yet all of it) from France. And although Louis XIV was permitted to make his grandson King of Spain it was on condition that France and Spain would never become one country under one ruler.

But this war had not only cost thousands of human lives, it had also cost money. For the sake of his glory Louis XIV had almost ruined France. Yet he continued to live in greater luxury than any other monarch, he was still *le Roi Soleil,* the Sun-King, who said, *"L'état, c'est moi."*

19. Versailles

Louis XIV simply commanded his parliament, the Estates General, to increase the taxes because he wanted a new palace, and squashed any objections by his words: "I am the state."

There was already a large royal palace in Paris, but this was not good enough for the Sun-King. He wanted another palace outside Paris, a palace surrounded by great parks, and, as it was his wish, the new Palace of Versailles was built just outside Paris in 1682.

It is a magnificent palace and even today no visitor to Paris will miss the opportunity to go and see it. The palace is so large that when the King was in residence there, ten thousand people — noblemen and their servants — lived in it. All the noblemen had their own private rooms, and there are, of course, enormous halls where they came together and where the King gave audience. The walls and ceilings are covered with pictures painted by the best artists of France. Big chandeliers (candle-holders for hundreds of candles) hang from the ceilings, and these chandeliers are made of solid silver. There are also chairs made of solid silver and every piece of furniture — tables, cupboards, beds — is a work of art, carved by craftsmen and inlaid with gold and silver, and there is the famous Hall of Mirrors that looks endless.

The vast grounds which surround the Palace of Versailles are just as impressive. The lawns are all laid out in perfect squares and rectangles and so all roads and paths run absolutely straight. Louis XIV and his gardeners had a passion for improving on nature and so even the trees at Versailles are not allowed to grow naturally but are, to this day, cut to regular shapes — cones, pyramids — so that they look like examples from geometry books.

All over these enormous gardens of Versailles there are statues and also many fountains which used to play continuously at the time of Louis XIV. Nowadays the fountains only flow on special national holidays — because it is too expensive to keep them going all the time — but for Louis XIV expense did not matter and the fountains sprayed water day and night, all the year.

Life inside the palace was just as strictly and stiffly regulated as the lawns and trees: how noblemen of equal rank greeted each other, how lords and ladies of different rank greeted each other, how each rank had to greet the King, how one walked, or sat down, and the eating and drinking and dancing, and how one dressed or played cards — it was all in accordance with strict rules called *etiquette*.

It was part of these strict rules that the highest noblemen of France, lords and dukes acted as personal servants to the King; — no ordinary servants were allowed to attend to the King but only men of noble blood.

Let us begin in the morning, with the "getting up," in French *le lever*. It sounds incredible, but this getting up was a great ceremony. At eight o'clock, the time when the King woke up, a duke presented him with his slippers and a prince handed him his dressing-gown. Then two noblemen brought him his prayer book and the King was left alone a few minutes to say his morning prayers.

Then a number of noblemen were allowed to be present while the King was shaved by a barber (who was not a nobleman). When the shaving was over, they all left and a new batch of noblemen came to help the King to dress.

Only the King's own brother had the privilege of handing him his shirt, then a lesser lord gave him his breeches (knee-length trousers), and another prince handed him his wig. Two noblemen (each holding one sleeve) helped the King into his coat, two others put his shoes on his feet, and there were still other noblemen to bring him his hat and gloves, and walking stick and a handkerchief.

In all this ceremony there is no mentioning of a wash — because neither the King nor his noblemen either washed or took a bath, ever. They used perfumes, scent, to hide the smell of their unwashed bodies.

Then at meal times it was again lords and noblemen who each served a different course to the King and the royal family;

and there was one nobleman who had the special duty of handing the King a napkin as often as it was needed — which was quite often as the King, like everyone in those days, used only a knife and his fingers.

The meals of His Majesty, Louis XIV, were enormous; for his midday meal he used to eat four large plates of soup, a whole pheasant or duck, two large helpings of ham, then came a plate of mutton, then four or five hard boiled eggs, and finally came cakes and fruit.

The morning — that is the time between *le lever* and lunch — was the time when the King attended to the business of government: he saw his ministers, dictated letters and received ambassadors of foreign countries.

But no such serious matters were allowed to disturb the afternoon or evening. The afternoon was given to the King's favourite sport: hunting. And for the evening there was again a complete change of dress — with the same ceremony as in the morning. All the courtiers too had to change and appear in evening clothes of silk or cloth of gold. The evening's entertainment was usually dancing and gambling and lasted till one o'clock at night. Then the King went to bed and his undressing was again attended and helped by chosen noblemen.

The cut and style of the dresses worn by lords and ladies changed continuously according to the whims and fancies of the King. But whatever the courtiers wore became immediately the fashion — first in Versailles, then in Paris, then in France and soon in the rest of the world. If Louis XIV decided one day to wear lace at his shirt-cuffs, a few months later every man in Europe and in America (who could afford it) wore lace on his cuffs.

The thousands of courtiers — the noble lords and ladies who surrounded the King and served him on hand and foot — competed with one another in flattering him, and went to any length to amuse and to please him.

At one time Louis XIV stayed as a guest with one of his noblemen, the Duke d'Autin. The King looked out of the splendid room given to him and mentioned to his host that the trees of a forest in the distance rather spoiled the fine view one had

from that room. The next morning as the King looked out —
the whole forest had disappeared. The peasants of the Duke had
worked all night to cut down and remove the trees which had
displeased His Majesty.

You can imagine that keeping not only the King and the royal
family but a whole royal court of thousands of noblemen in
such luxury cost a lot of money. And where did all this money
come from? From the peasants of France. They did not live in
luxury, they lived in dirty hovels, they walked about in rags, they
were hungry and often near starvation, but it was their hard
work which had to provide the King and his court with the luxuries, the fine dresses, the enormous meals, the splendid palace.

The Royal Tax Collectors were officials whose duty it was to
raise the money from the people. They came, accompanied by
soldiers — and if a peasant did not have the money for the tax
ready, the soldiers took away his last cow or sheep or even his
plough. The fact that this peasant would not have any money
the next year either — as he could not till his land — did not
matter. Not did it matter if he and his family died of hunger: the
peasant, like the courtiers, existed only for the King's pleasure.

So, with the reign of Louis XIV, there begins a time in France
when a few thousand people — the King and his court — lived
in fantastic luxury, while millions of ordinary people became
poorer and poorer.

But it was not only the luxuries of Versailles the peasants had
to pay for, but also the vainglorious wars Louis XIV started. It
was the peasants' taxes which paid for the weapons and guns and
for the soldiers' pay, and it was the peasants' sons who marched
and fought and died in battle for the glory of Louis XIV.

20. Banking

The extravagance, the sheer waste of money at the court of Louis XIV, in contrast to the plight of the peasant population, might lead one to think that this is a period in the history of France which people recall only with shame. But it is not so, because it is also a time in which some very great Frenchmen lived — great painters, architects, poets and playwrights. Just as the time of Queen Elizabeth was a time of great Englishmen like Drake, Raleigh, Shakespeare, one hundred years later in the time of Louis XIV, there were great Frenchmen.

One of the great men of that time was Molière, who wrote comedies, funny plays which are still performed today in France, as we perform Shakespeare's plays. There is one play *(Le Malade Imaginaire)* in which Molière makes fun of a man who is so fussy about his health that he imagines he suffers from every possible and impossible illness. In another play *(Le Bourgeois Gentilhomme)* he makes fun of an ordinary man who tries to imitate the manners of noble courtiers. They are plays one can still enjoy today.

It was no merit of Louis XIV that gave rise to such great painters and writers and architects existing in his time, but he did support them and paid them and gave them work to do, because of course, it helped to glorify himself.

But for the poor hungry peasants of that time, the clever plays, the beautiful paintings, the splendid palace of Versailles meant very little. One day a howling mob of hungry people in rags surrounded the Palace of Versailles, shouting, "Bread, Bread, give us bread!" But the soldiers of the Palace Guard came and drove them away. The people did not forget how little the King cared for their poverty and suffering when Louis XIV died in 1715, the mob of Paris shouted curses at the funeral procession. The common people of France were glad at the news that *le Roi Soleil* had died.

Louis XIV had outlived his son and grandson, they both died before him — and his great-grandson was only five years old at the death of *le Roi Soleil*. The little boy's uncle, Philip, Duke of Orleans, was appointed as "Regent," as it is called, to rule temporarily, in the name of the King, but not as King. However, Philip, the Regent, had been a courtier of *le Roi Soleil* for too long to care for anything but festivities and amusements, and his only worry now was where to find money for his own pleasures and those of the court.

It was at this time that John Law, a Scotsman from Edinburgh, brought a new idea to France.

France had colonies; she still had a large part of Canada as well as a part of North America called Louisiana (in honour of Louis XIV). These colonies could be developed — so said John Law — and they could bring money to France. But first money had to be put in, men had to be sent out, with ships, arms, equipment. In time though, every pound spent on the colonies would come back twofold and threefold.

And all one had to do was — not tax the people — but *borrow* the money from them, with the promise to pay it back later when the colonies flourished, and every man who lent the Government one pound could be certain to receive two or three pounds later, in return.

It seemed a wonderful idea, the Regent Philip agreed and John Law opened a bank in Paris in 1716. This bank offered the people papers which were called bank notes. If you wanted such a bank note for one pound you had to pay the bank a gold coin worth one pound. But — incredibly — this same banknote would later on, be worth two pounds, or three pounds — or even ten pounds which would be repaid in gold again, within a few years. Nowadays people buy "shares" in a company — it is the same thing. You buy a share for £1 — and you hope and expect that the company will make profits and these profits (a share of them) will be paid to you and make the £1 worth £1.10, £1.50 or even £5. Sometimes it happens, and sometimes it doesn't. It is a gamble.

In those days, however, it was something quite new, and people fell for it. John Law himself believed honestly that the gamble would come off — that the French colonies would become very profitable. And the French people believed it too. The peasants had no money, but in the cities and towns of France, people had money, people had savings — and they came in their thousands and bought John Law's banknotes. In fact, there was soon a trade in these banknotes. A man who bought a banknote for £1 could sell it to another man a month later for £2, because that other man now expected to get much more for it. And all those who gave up their little savings for these bits of paper saw themselves as millionaires in a year or two.

But, of course, it was all a dream. The French colonies did not produce such great profits, and certainly not as fast as people expected. A few clever people did not wait very long — they soon came to John Law and said: "Here are our £1 notes, we want as promised £2 or £3 in gold," and they got it. But, of course, there was only enough real money in the Bank to satisfy the first few who came, and no money at all for those who came later, they could not even get their £1 back. There was a panic: everybody wanted to sell banknotes, and no one wanted to buy them, and the notes became worthless.

Hundreds of thousands of people had lost all their savings and John Law had to flee from France. He had not made any money for himself, but the idea had not worked and the people blamed him for it. He died in poverty in Italy in 1729.

But the idea of bank notes — of giving people paper instead of gold coins, this idea was later taken up by all governments, and in our time gold coins have disappeared altogether.

The people of France had no love for the Regent Philip who had let John Law start this disastrous experiment. And they rejoiced in 1722 when the true successor, the great-grandson of the *Roi Soleil* became King Louis XV at the age of thirteen.

He was a handsome young boy, and no king had a better welcome; the people called him *le bien aimée*, "the well-beloved." They expected of him he would put things right and do something about the widespread poverty.

But Louis XV had a most unfortunate upbringing: he had been spoiled and petted, he had been flattered and praised and fussed over, and as a result he knew only one rule of life: his own pleasure, his own satisfaction.

His private tutors — instead of teaching him — played cards with him, because he liked it better than work. And as soon as he was old enough to hunt he gave up his lessons altogether. What need had a king to learn anything? Once Louis XV was crowned King he found the job of governing France just as boring as lessons — and left that tedious job to others.

At the age of seventeen he was married to a Polish princess — but he got soon tired of his wife and found one of the court ladies more attractive. The name of this lady was Madame de Pompadour. She was beautiful and clever, and ambitious. She wanted to rule France, and lazy, spineless Louis XV was only too pleased to let her.

And so it came that France was ruled by the King's mistress, Madame de Pompadour. Louis XV said yes to all she wanted, put his signature to any document she put before him, and took no interest in what happened to France or in France. He gave his time entirely to amusements, festivities, games, and suffered only from one thing: boredom.

21. Louis XV and Frederick the Great

Louis XV had been completely spoiled from early childhood. No effort had ever been demanded of him, no wish had ever been denied to him, so he grew up into a lazy good-for-nothing who was, however, King of France — a king with absolute power. And as Louis XV was too lazy to rule and to shoulder the burden and worries of government, he left his absolute power in the hands of his lady-love, Madame de Pompadour. You can see how the upbringing of a king, specially this utterly ineffectual upbringing could influence the fate of a whole nation.

At the same time as Louis XV there was another king whose upbringing was the very opposite: it was a harsh and strict upbringing. But this king is given a designation few kings are ever given — he is called "the Great" and so belongs to the illustrious company of Alexander, Charlemagne (French for Charles the Great) and Alfred.

This king was Frederick the Great of Prussia. Prussia was a little kingdom in the North of Germany and, in theory, the kings of Prussia owed obedience to the Emperor of Germany who had his capital in Vienna. But this was only in theory. In reality, the little kingdoms of Germany — Prussia, Bavaria, Saxony — were quite independent and even made war against the Emperor, if and when, they wanted to.

Frederick the Great's father, Frederick William was a rough-mannered man who despised elegant clothes and fine manners — the lifestyle of the French court. Frederick William had quite a different ambition: to have the best fighting men, the best soldiers in the world.

The idea of army drill was taken to the limits by Frederick William: Soldiers should stand "to attention" as stiff as ramrods; whole regiments should march, present arms, or turn about like one man and with the precision of machines. His soldiers were truly trained in this manner, and once a soldier was used to obeying commands as though he were a machine, he would also obey in battle, without thinking, even if it cost him his life. The soldiers of Prussia were drilled for absolute obedience.

But King Frederick William also demanded the same obedience, the same discipline, from his son, Frederick.

Frederick did not enjoy this at all; young Frederick did not like the rigid discipline and the rough manners of his father. He preferred the fine manners, the elegant fashions of France. And when his father made him an officer in the Prussian army at the age of sixteen, Frederick made plans with another officer to run away, to flee from Prussia and to go to France.

But the plan was uncovered, and the old King would not tolerate such disobedience. The officer who had been willing to help Prince Frederick was condemned to death, and Frederick had to watch a squad of soldiers put his friend against a wall and shoot him.

It was a terrible experience for young Frederick — but it taught him that there was no escape from his duties and from obedience to his father's wishes. He became an efficient officer and, later, an outstanding general. But this experience of seeing his best friend shot also made him a hard man, a man who had little feeling for others.

Many years later, in a battle, when Frederick's soldiers were mown down by heavy cannon-fire, their iron discipline broke and they turned to flee, Frederick shouted furiously at them "You dogs, do you want to live for ever?" The men turned round and continued the attack.

So, when the old King, Frederick William, died in 1740 and Frederick became King of Prussia, this young King was a very different person from the soft, lazy and spoiled Louis XV who had never known any hardship in his life.

Of course, both kinds of upbringing are wrong — the merciless discipline imposed on Frederick and the soft petting and spoiling which ruined Louis. It is, really, the same polarity as there was between Puritans and Cavaliers. Frederick became a man one can respect but not like, and Louis XV was a person one could like for his charm but not respect.

As soon as Frederick had become King of Prussia he wanted to use the well-drilled army that was at his command. At the time the Emperor of Germany had died and was succeeded by his daughter, Maria Theresa, Empress of Germany and Austria.

Frederick thought that his own Prussia too small and he could make it bigger by taking a slice away from the lands ruled by the Empress Maria Theresa. After all, she was "only a woman" and this should make it easier, so Frederick declared war on the Empress.

But it was not such an easy war as Frederick had expected, for Louis XV of France — or rather Madame de Pompadour who made the decisions — came into the war on the side of Maria Theresa.

Britain, on the other hand, decided to come in on the side of Frederick. And then Russia, too, joined in, on the side of Maria Theresa.

So there was Prussia and Britain on one side, France, Russia, Austria on the other, and the whole of Europe was thrown into war and bloodshed.

And this was not only fought in Europe; on the high seas British and French ships fought each other; in North America English and French colonists fought each other and the Native American tribes were brought in on both sides; it was really a world war.

It was also a long war — a war that lasted for seven years (1756–63), thus it is called the Seven Years' War. It cost innumerable lives. It also cost, like all wars, a great deal of money. And, of all the nations which took part in this war, France could least afford to spend money on war. But all this did not worry Louis XV who carried on with his pleasures and festivities and entertainments in the Palace of Versailles. He left politics to Madame de Pompadour and the fighting to his generals.

Frederick of Prussia at least commanded his own troops and shared with them the hardship of war, and it was due to his generalship and iron determination that, in the end, against the great armies of Austria, Russia, France, the small but well-trained army of Prussia won. The Seven Years' War ended with victory for Frederick. It also ended with victory for Britain which took the remaining parts of Canada from France.

But France was now worse off than ever before; she had lost Canada, she had lost thousands of soldiers killed in battle, and she had wasted vast amounts of money for nothing.

Yet all this may not have come upon France if Louis XV had been brought up differently, or if Frederick of Prussia had been brought up differently.

22. The Count of Saint Germain

You can see from the examples of Louis XV and Frederick the Great of Prussia that their upbringing influenced the fate of whole nations. France lost her colonies and became poorer than ever before, but Prussia became the most powerful of the German states. But it was surely wrong that the fate of millions, their prosperity or poverty, should depend on the character, the strength or weakness of one man. In ancient Egypt people had, indeed, accepted good kings or bad kings as the will of the gods; in ancient Rome people still accepted good Caesars or weak and evil ones as the will of the gods. In the early Middle Ages the Christian kings were still believed to be the instruments of God's will. But the *new age* — the age that began with Leonardo and Columbus and Luther — this new age could not look up to kings with awe and respect, and, in the long run, people would not let a single man — just because he was a King — make decisions about the fate of millions. The time for this absolute power of kings was past.

There were people at that time who gave much thought to this question. The absolute power of kings has to go — but should it be swept away in chaos and bloodshed, or would it not be better if this great change came peacefully, step by step?

While most people, if they worry about the future at all, only worry about their own well-being, or that of their families; in contrast, there were people who were concerned about the future of Europe and of mankind as a whole and they wanted to help so that progress and change should come without great suffering and bloodshed.

In the Middle Ages the alchemists searched for the secret of the Philosophers' Stone, the stone which could change base metals into gold, which could give a long life, which could cure illness. They were the "true alchemists" — and only a truly selfless person could ever join the secret brotherhood of the true alchemists. The sign of this secret brotherhood was a black cross from which red roses grew. Now this secret brotherhood of the Rosicrucians decided to try to avert the terror and bloodshed they saw coming in Europe, and especially France.

In the year 1760, during the Seven Years' War, a strange man appeared in Paris. He called himself the Count of Saint Germain, but, as he said himself, it was not his real name and no one has ever found out who he really was and what his real name was.

This strange man, the Count of Saint Germain, seemed to be immensely rich, his exquisite clothes were adorned with great diamonds and rubies, he gave great parties and banquets for hundreds of people, and the noble lords and ladies of France flocked to the invitations of this strange man who seemed to have unlimited money, though no one could make out where his money came from as he had no business, no estates, farms, houses.

What was even stranger was that he looked like a man of about fifty years of age, but an old lady who came to one of his parties swore she had seen him when she was a young girl, some forty years earlier in Italy, and he had then looked just the same — a man of about fifty years of age. So imagine how puzzled people were by this mysterious stranger who called himself the Count of Saint Germain.

It is no wonder that the King, Louis XV, heard rumours of this stranger and became curious to meet him, and so the Count of Saint Germain was invited to the Court, to the Palace of Versailles. The King was greatly impressed by Saint Germain, by the dignity and wisdom with which he spoke and by the great knowledge he showed in science, in history, in every subject one could talk about.

One day King Louis showed Saint Germain a large diamond which was, however, not very valuable because it had a flaw, a dark spot in it. Saint Germain said: "Let me have it, I will return it to you without flaw, without the dark spot in a few weeks." And so he did — yet no one knows how he could remove a dark spot from inside a diamond. No one can do it today.

It is not surprising that the King became very friendly with this mysterious stranger. It is also not surprising that Madame de Pompadour and other French noblemen became jealous and began to hate this man who came from nowhere, who was, perhaps, not even of noble blood but was so much in the King's favour.

And then came a day when the Count of Saint Germain spoke alone to the King about France and said: "This war with Prussia will ruin France if it goes on for another few years. And if there is hunger and poverty in the land, it may well lead to a revolution, to bloodshed and civil war. If you want to avoid this, Your Majesty, you must end the war with Prussia right now."

King Louis sighed and said: "Madame de Pompadour and her war-minister are quite determined to go on with the war, they are certain we are going to win. And, frankly, I have not the strength of will to start a row and a long argument with her and the minister. I have left the worries of government to her and I can't quite suddenly change this arrangement which, after all, saves me all the bother.

And then the Count of Saint Germain said: "If you dare not openly go against the wishes of Madame de Pompadour, let me go secretly in your name and try to make peace with Prussia. Once I have a peace-treaty, Madame de Pompadour and her minister will not object any longer, and, perhaps, they will realize that this is the best for all concerned."

Well, the King agreed half-heartedly and gave the Count of Saint Germain permission to go in secret to Holland which was a neutral country and meet the Prussian ambassador there and discuss a peace-treaty between Prussia and France with him.

If this plan of the Count of Saint Germain had succeeded, the history of France, the history of whole Europe would have been different. But things did not go according to plan.

Madame de Pompadour and the War Minister had spies who told them that there were strange goings-on in Holland between Saint Germain and the Prussian ambassador. Madame de Pompadour went to Louis, told him she knew he was doing something behind her back and demanded an explanation. When Louis told her of his secret arrangement with Saint Germain, she was furious. "France is going to win the war, there is no reason to ask Prussia for peace, and France must not let down her allies — Russia and the Austrian Empire. The whole stupid plan had to be stopped right away."

And Louis, weak as he was, gave in. A message was sent to Holland that the Count of Saint Germain had no permission and no authority from the King of France to discuss a peace-treaty and that was the end of the discussions. The war went on for another four years and ended with France defeated and poorer then ever before.

The Count of Saint Germain disappeared as suddenly as he had come upon the scene. Some people met him in London a year later, and then he was gone. It is not known where he went and when and where he died.

He had come as a messenger of the secret brotherhood of the Cross and the Roses to save France from the terrors that were in store for her, but jealousy and vanity, and the weak character of Louis XV had ruined his attempt to save France.

23. Rousseau, Voltaire and the Aristocrats

The story of the Count of Saint Germain shows how the secret brotherhood of the Rosicrucians tried to guide the new age that had begun with the age of discovery, so that all the changes this new age would bring should come as blessings and not through chaos and disasters. But this secret brotherhood had no soldiers, no power to enforce its wishes, it could only work where there was good will — and in the case of the Count of Saint Germain the attempt to help France failed.

But there were other ways in which the secret brotherhood could work. For instance, it could try to bring into the world new ideas. The old ideas about the divine rights of kings were doomed to go, in some countries sooner, in other countries later, but they would go. If the old ideas went, however, new ideas had to come. At times this secret brotherhood worked to bring new ideas into the world.

There was a young man, a writer, whose name was Jean Jacques Rousseau (1712–78). He later became famous, but at that time he was still unknown. Now the French Academy in Paris — a college of the most learned men of France, announced a competition for the best essay on the "Blessings of Civilization." The competitors were supposed to write about the terrible kind of life amongst savages, or in ancient times when our own ancestors were primitive people who lived in caves, and then the essay should describe how much better people lived when civilization came, houses, cities, inventions and orderly government.

Of course, many writers all over France were keen to take part in this competition; not only was there a sum of money as reward for the best essay, it would also be a great honour to win the first prize. Jean Jacques Rousseau also wanted to write an essay in the hope to win the prize. He was giving much thought to what he should write and how he should write it — and he used to go for long walks to collect his thoughts. Like many people he could think better if he went for a walk. On one of these walks he sat down on a bench and a stranger, a man whom he had never seen before, sat down beside him and started a conversation.

During the course of this talk, Rousseau told the man that he was working on this essay on the "Blessings of Civilization."

"Well," said the stranger, "I think it would be much more original if you were to write the opposite. Show in your essay, how unnatural, how artificial life has become through civilization — and that human happiness does not come through civilization but from living in accordance with nature. Is not the beauty of a mountain, of a sunrise, more wonderful than all the rules and regulations which we call civilization? If you really knew the so-called savages you might find more dignity, more wisdom and more happiness amongst them than in the so-called civilized nations. Think about it."

And with these words the stranger left. Rousseau never saw him again, but the ideas of the stranger were like seeds which took root in his own mind. He never wrote the essay on the "Blessings of Civilization," but he wrote many books in which he praised the beauty of nature when it is unspoiled by man.

Before Rousseau no one had ever written about climbing mountains for pleasure or enjoying a walk in a forest. It was through the books of Rousseau that the beauty of nature was popularized.

But Rousseau also wrote about government. Is it natural for men to have kings, to obey the laws of kings? No, answered Rousseau — man is born with natural rights which no king can take from him. Kings and royalty and noblemen with special privileges and rights are not natural — and what is *not* natural is wrong.

The books of Rousseau became famous, they were read by thousands in France and soon in other countries of Europe and in America. These books opened people's eyes, and they began to think about government as they had never thought before.

It all began with that stranger who met Rousseau on his walk. But this meeting was no accident. The stranger was a member of that secret brotherhood that wanted to guide people to new ideas.

But Rousseau was not the only writer of that time who made people think. Another Frenchman of that time was Voltaire (1694–1778). Voltaire was a man of great wit who showed what was wrong with France in his books, what was wrong with its government and wrong with its rich, spoiled noblemen — by making fun of it all.

People laughed when they read Voltaire's books, but they laughed at things they had formerly respected: the authority of the King, the privileges of the noblemen, the power of the Catholic Church. They laughed — and as they laughed, they lost their respect for those in authority. Unfortunately, in his books Voltaire made fun of religion altogether, not only of the Church and wicked priests.

And through his books many people lost their faith in God altogether and became enemies of religion.

The books of Voltaire, like those of Rousseau, influenced and changed the ideas of millions of people all over Europe, but especially in France. People looked upon the Church, the King, the noblemen with new eyes; the old authority was gone and people saw their rulers and masters in a new light, the light of reason. That's why this time is called the period of Enlightenment. And in this enlightenment — in the light of reason — the King and his courtiers and noblemen did not look as if they deserved the respect which they had enjoyed before.

Let us try to get a picture of life in France at that time.

The nobility — or as they are called, the aristocrats — the dukes, counts, barons, earls, lived a life of ease and pleasure; they owned great estates on which the peasants worked and toiled to provide their noble masters with the money they needed to live in style.

It was quite unthinkable that an aristocrat ever did any physical work or went into business. An aristocrat could become a courtier of the King, or even a minister, and many of them became officers in the army. It would have been a disgrace for an aristocrat to own a shop or to become a carpenter or even to be a doctor though. There was, however, no need for the aristocrats to enter any of the despised professions as their estates provided the money they needed. And, to make life even sweeter for them, the aristocrats did not have to pay any taxes. It was the common people who paid the taxes which kept the royal court in luxury. No wonder these aristocrats, lords and ladies, had a lot of time and money to spend on their clothes.

By this time, from about 1700 onwards, men no longer wore wigs with curly hair. They still wore wigs, but the wigs had rolls on either side and ended at the back in a pig-tail decorated with a large black bow.

This wig was no longer in any natural colour but was powdered white. People's houses had special powder cabinets where servants used clouds of flour to whiten their masters' wigs.

The clothes men wore were colourful: blue, fawn, pink, and there was fine lace worn at the neck and on the wrists. A three-cornered hat, and a thin sword, completed a gentleman's dress.

Ladies' dress was even more elaborate. A lady's hair-do was piled up high on the head and so complicated that a woman had to spend more than an hour every morning — with the help of several maids — to get her hair right. The skirts were enormous, bulging out widely from the hips by means of a wire-structure underneath.

Both, ladies and gentlemen, took pride in graceful manners and graceful movements. A man's bow, a woman's curtsey, were practised and practised endlessly to make them beautiful.

Every gesture and every movement was the result of endless practice. To talk, sit down or stand up naturally as we do, would have seemed to these people crude and barbaric. Even taking "snuff" (which was then a great fashion) and blowing his nose afterwards, was something that had to be done gracefully.

But the men who took so much trouble over their clothes and graceful manners were not weaklings. They were tough and they did not wear their thin swords (foils) for nothing. The slightest provocation — a real or imaginary insult — and a duel followed.

It was a great life for the aristocrats, but not for the greater part of the population. It was a miserable life for the peasant who had no rights at all, not even the right to leave the service of his master. He belonged to the farm like the trees that grew on it. They lived in hovels, together with pigs and goats and chickens. They wore tattered rags and they had no education whatsoever.

But, between the aristocrats and the miserable peasants there was a middle-class, the burghers, or bourgeois. This middle-class, the bourgeois, wanted to change this shameful system.

24. The American War of Independence

We looked at the three "classes" into which France was divided at that time: the nobility or aristocrats, who had rights and privileges — even the privilege of not paying any taxes; the peasants who had neither rights nor privileges and lived in poverty and ignorance; and between these two classes the middle-class or bourgeoisie. The bourgeois were mainly concentrated in the cities; they were the artisans, carpenters, tailors, the shopkeepers and merchants, the doctors and lawyers.

On the one hand, these bourgeois copied the manners and fashions of the aristocrats; although the bourgeois were heavily taxed, they also made money in their trades and professions and they used their money to dress and live like the aristocrats whom they envied.

But the bourgeois were also educated people. It was the bourgeois who read the books of Rousseau and Voltaire and who learned from these books to regard the whole class-system of France as something wicked and stupid. Amongst the middle-class, amongst the bourgeois, the books of the "enlightenment" became like gun-powder needing only a spark to set off an explosion.

However, the first explosion did not come in France, it came in far-off North America where the theories of Rousseau and Voltaire were put into practice for the first time.

In the Seven Years' War, Britain had fought on the side of Prussia against France. And the English colonists in America had come faithfully to the aid of the "old country" and had fought against the French colonists in Canada. But those British colonists in America were poorly rewarded for their loyalty.

The English general who came over to America to command the colonists showed quite openly his contempt for the rough "colonials" as he called them. There was one colonial officer, George Washington, who fought gallantly and bravely, developing a shrewd knowledge of warfare. Although he had wanted to become a professional soldier, when the Seven Years' War was over, he left the army because he was disgusted with the way the men from England had looked down on him and the other colonials. George Washington left the army and devoted himself to managing a large farm he had in Virginia.

But the contempt of the English for the American colonials showed itself also in other ways. The Seven Years' War had cost a lot of money and the Government Treasury was empty, so the King of England, George III, and the British Government decided that the only way to fill it up again, was by raising the taxes.

That worked in Britain; the people in Britain paid the new taxes dutifully — after all, it was their own Members of Parliament, the Government they had elected, that had decided these taxes were necessary. But the colonials in America did not feel like that at all. The American colonials had no Member of Parliament in London, they were not represented. And they complained. They complained that there should be "no taxation without representation." This meant, "If we have no say in the Government, we will not pay taxes imposed by the Government."

The Americans sent one of their best men to England to plead for their rights. His name was Benjamin Franklin. Franklin came from a poor family, most of what he had learned he had taught himself. When he read a book, he first read a few pages, then he closed the book, and wrote down what he remembered, and then he compared his writing with the book to see if he had left out anything. In this way he had made himself a famous writer and a man greatly respected by his fellow-Americans. He was also interested in science, experimented with electricity and invented the lightning conductor. This was the man the Americans sent to London to speak for them. But neither George III nor the ministers of the English Government had much patience for the American complaints and Benjamin Franklin had to go back to America without having achieved anything.

And soon after his return something happened to make things worse between the colonials and England.

The colonials — who were, after all English and Scots — liked to drink tea. And when the London Government put a tax on their tea (again without asking if the colonials agreed) the Americans were very angry. The tax itself was not much, but it was a matter of principle.

The Government wanted to show the colonials that they had to pay if London said so, whether they agreed or not. And the Americans wanted to show that they were not willing to pay one penny unless they had agreed to do so. It was a matter of principle on both sides.

And so, one day, in 1773, three ships carrying cases of tea arrived in the American port of Boston. But before the cases could be unloaded a gang of young men, disguised as native Americans, boarded the ships and threw all the tea-cases into the sea. The Americans call this event the "Boston Tea-Party." It was no more than a prank, but a prank that led to war.

The English Government sent troops to America to frighten the Americans into obedience. But this only had the opposite effect, it roused the colonists to fight for their rights.

The Americans called a great meeting in Philadelphia — and at this meeting or Congress they proclaimed the ideas of Rousseau, the natural rights of man. The answer of the British Government was to send yet more soldiers to America. But now the Americans took to arms and at the small town of Lexington in Massachussets, there came the first battle which, to their great surprise the English "Redcoats" lost.

Soon the fighting spread, and the Americans elected George Washington as their general and leader the man who had proved his gallantry and knowledge of warfare.

It was a sad time when English-speaking people fought each other in America. And, as always, other nations came in on either side. German troops came to America to fight for the British, and French volunteers led by a nobleman, Lafayette, came to fight on the side of the Americans.

As the war progressed, the Americans decided that they wanted more than just fair treatment from the London

Government, they wanted complete independence with their own government in America.

On the July 4, 1776 the delegates meeting in Philadelphia proclaimed the British colony to be the independent United States of America. July 4 is still celebrated in America as Independence Day, a national holiday to commemorate the famous Declaration of Independence. The new country was not going to have a king, it was not to have any noblemen and aristocrats, it was a land where all men should have equal rights, the natural rights of man. They would elect in freedom their own government and president.

In the American Declaration of Independence, the ideas of the Enlightenment, the ideas of Rousseau and Voltaire, were put into practice for the first time.

George III and the British Government were not at all pleased to lose the American colony, and they continued the war against the "colonials." But General Washington had made a fighting force of his untrained rough colonials that could beat the trained and drilled British Redcoats. The French volunteers under Lafayette also fought gallantly, and the British could not win against people who fought for their freedom.

Moreover, in Britain, there were a good many people — even amongst members of the Government — who were in sympathy with the Americans. And amongst the common people of England there was little enthusiasm for a war against colonists who were English and many of whom still had relatives in England. And so, after eight years the War of Independence came to an end. In 1783 peace was made, and it was Benjamin Franklin who signed the peace-treaty in which Britain recognized her former colony as an independent "sovereign" state. And it was George Washington who became the first president of the new country, the United States of America.

In the American War of Independence the ideas of human rights had won their first victory.

25. Louis XVI.
The Three Estates

In the history of ancient times one hears mainly about kings and noblemen, and even the crusades were still lead and commanded by noble knights and kings. Joan of Arc was, perhaps, the first commoner to lead armies and to change the course of history. But then, with the beginning of the new age, the great men came from the middle-classes; Leonardo, Columbus, Galilei. But the middle-classes could not only produce artists, explorers, scientists, they could also produce statesmen and generals, as Cromwell had shown in England, and as Washington and Franklin showed in America a century later. You can see that we have come to the time when the middle-class, the "bourgeois" became the people who made history. And the American War of Independence was a victory for "bourgeois," for middle-class people who had taken up arms to fight for their rights.

In 1774 while this War of Independence was still in progress, Louis XV died in France (Madame de Pompadour had died before him). But few Frenchmen had any tears for a king who had remained spoiled all his life without a thought to his responsibilities as ruler of the nation. Louis' son had died before him, so it was his grandson, Louis XVI of France, who became King at the age of nineteen.

Young Louis XVI was not madly ambitious for glory, like Louis XIV, *le Roi Soleil,* nor did he care for senseless amusements like Louis XV, he was a much better man who took his duties as King of France very seriously. But France was by then in a terrible plight and only a man of great genius might have found a way to solve the urgent problems of the country. But Louis XVI was not a genius, he was not even clever, and the only thing he was really good at was his hobby: making iron-locks. In his spare-time he hammered happily in a little workshop rigged up for him at Versailles — but this innocent hobby was no help in solving the problems of France.

Nor was his wife — whom he loved dearly — a great help. Queen Marie Antoinette was an Austrian princess, the daughter of Maria Theresa. She was pretty and lively, she liked fine clothes and gay parties, but she was not clever. Marie Antoinette, too, had a hobby. You see, by this time Rousseau's ideas about "natural" life had become fashionable, even amongst the aristocrats. And what could be nicer than to have a bit of "natural" life in between the ceremony and glitter of the court.

And so, Queen Marie Antoinette had a little farm complete with a cow-shed arranged for her in the vast parks of Versailles. And she and her court ladies would dress up as peasant-girls, and go down to the little farm and milk the cows and sing country-songs — and pretend they were country girls for a couple of hours.

Poor Marie Antoinette had no idea that the real peasants of France, hardworking, hungry, and in rags, looked at her "game" as an insult, as if she was making fun of their misery and poverty. But Marie Antoinette was only thoughtless and silly.

There is a story (I don't know if it is true) that when Marie Antoinette was told one day that peasants were rebellious because they had no bread, she asked astonished "But, if they have no bread, why don't they eat cakes?"

France was in a state when such a king and such a queen were of no use at all!

The Seven Years' War had left France desperately poor, and then France had fought another war against Britain to help America, and this war had also cost money and brought no benefits to France.

The working people — the peasants and the middle-classes — had been taxed and taxed until they could not be taxed any more, but the rich aristocrats as well as the bishops, who had money and vast estates, were not be taxed at all. Since the Middle Ages the Church and the noblemen had been exempt from taxes, and it seemed as if the time had come that the Church and the noblemen, too, should make a contribution to the taxes. But the bishops and noblemen of France were not willing to give up their ancient privileges to be free from taxation.

And then in 1788 there was a terribly bad harvest in France followed by an abnormally long and hard winter. There was a disastrous food-shortage all over France, and the only way to save thousands from starvation was to buy corn from other countries; but to buy corn — thousands of tons — money was required, and there was no money in the treasury for such a big purchase.

In this desperate situation Louis XVI could and should have ordered the noblemen and the Church to pay taxes, but he failed to take this radical action. Instead he called a meeting of the Estates General, the "three estates." The bishops of the Church were the first estate, the aristocrats were the second estate, and the middle-class were the third estate. And all three "estates" sent their representatives to this meeting at Versailles in 1789.

Louis XVI hoped that at this meeting the three estates would find by agreement a way to solve the desperate problem of feeding the French people. But the only answer would have been for the Church and the aristocrats to give up their privilege and to pay taxes. And this was exactly what they did not want to do. There was a lot of bickering and argument — but no agreement on anything.

And then something quite unexpected happened. The "deputies" of the third estate declared that they stood for ninety-five per cent of the population, that they were therefore the true representatives of the French nation — and they were the true parliament of France and would make the laws which France needed.

They did not use the word "parliament" — they called it "National Assembly" but it meant the same thing. The deputies of the third estate simply declared they were going to make new laws, without asking the King, or the aristocracy or the bishops for agreement.

King Louis XVI had not expected that such a thing could happen in France, that commoners would take over government and make their own laws. He gave orders that the deputies should disband and go home. The bishops and noblemen obeyed — but the deputies of the commoners replied: "We are here by the will of the people and we shall not go unless we are forced by the bayonets of your soldiers."

Another king might have used soldiers against them, but

Louis XVI, up to the end of his life, wanted to avoid bloodshed. He did not send soldiers, and the National Assembly stayed and defied his orders.

In the meantime, Paris, which is only a short distance from Versailles, was in a fever of excitement. In the open squares, in the streets crowds of thousands listened to speakers who exhorted them to stand by their deputies and to come and fight for them if the King used force against them.

Suddenly there were rumours (quite false, of course) that the King had sent soldiers to arrest the deputies. It is quite certain that these rumours were spread deliberately by men who wanted a revolution against the King. And these rumours turned the exited crowds into an angry and howling mob. In one public square, a young man, Camille Desmoulins by name, jumped on a table, fired a pistol into the air and shouted: "To arms, citizens — fight for freedom!"

And like waves in a storm, the crowds surged through the streets of Paris, they plundered the shops of gunsmiths, they stole knives from butchers' shops, they stormed the Arsenal, the weapon-store of the French army.

It is quite certain that this crazy, howling, rioting mob was directed by people who knew exactly what they wanted all along — and used the rabble for their own purposes. And once the crowds were armed they surged to a huge prison-fortress in the East of Paris, called the Bastille.

The officer in charge of the Bastille wanted to avoid bloodshed. He offered to open the gates and to surrender the Bastille if he and his soldiers were allowed to leave unharmed. The promise was given — but as soon as the gates were opened the mob stormed in and killed the officer and his men without mercy. Then the mob with great cheers set free the seven prisoners they found in the jails of the Bastille. Five of them were common thieves, one was a madman and only one man claimed he was imprisoned without reason.

This storming of the Bastille on July 14, 1789 was the beginning of the French Revolution. It is still a national holiday in France.

26. Liberty – Equality – Fraternity

The French Revolution began with the storming of the Bastille, when a mad crowd, excited by false rumours, stormed the old prison-fortress for no good reason at all. It was a sudden explosion, this revolution, but the gun-powder which exploded was the ideas of Rousseau and Voltaire. For years and years these ideas had spread amongst the people. More and more Frenchmen had come to think of monarchy and of aristocracy as a swindle; as useless remnants of the past that should be swept away. Even amongst the aristocrats themselves there were many who sympathized with the new ideas, and who looked forward to a world without the old privileges.

Over many years revolutionary secret societies had been forming in France. In these secret societies men of high birth and commoners, lawyers, doctors and journalists came together and laid their plans to do away with the false things, with royalty and nobility as well as with the Church. And they also spoke in these secret meetings of the new order that should come after they had got rid of kings and aristocrats.

Again and again three words come up when they spoke of the future, three words which should bring a new and better order not only to France but to the mankind as a whole world. The first one who used these three words and explained their meaning was one of those unknown messengers of the secret brotherhood of Rosicrucians. These three words were: liberty, equality and brotherhood.

The meaning of these three words is this: In religion, in science, in art, there should be absolute *liberty* or freedom, everyone should be free to have their own opinion and to express it in words or in writing.

Human beings don't live in isolation, they live together with each other so there must be laws to regulate life together. But these laws must be the same for all, there cannot be special laws for the rich and other laws for the poor, or special laws for clever people and other laws for stupid ones. Before the law there must be *equality*.

But there is still the work we do, and in our work we depend on each other. The scientist in his laboratory needs the farmer who grows the food and they both need the iron-worker to fashion their tools for them. In the end all people need each other — and that is the *fraternity* or brotherhood of work.

In our thoughts we must have freedom, before the law, there must be equality, in our work there is — whether we are aware of it or not — brotherhood, for we all depend on other peoples' work as they depend on ours.

But these three — freedom, equality, brotherhood — must never get into the wrong place. A painter of little talent is, as a painter, not the equal of Leonardo. Or, if I have my own opinion about, let us say, music I don't have to change it for the sake of brotherhood, and agree with others. Freedom, equality and brotherhood each have their own place — and if any of them is put in the wrong place, the result is chaos.

This is what was originally said about the three ideas which should build a new order when the old order of kings and aristocracy had gone. But as time passed this original meaning of the three words was forgotten. When the conspirators who planned the French Revolution came together, they talked about freedom, equality and fraternity (or brotherhood) as if it did not matter where each belonged.

It was these conspirators, these plotters who roused the crowds by false rumours on July 14, 1789, who turned the mob against the Bastille and so started the French Revolution.

And it was these conspirators who proclaimed to the people that the nations of the world should no longer be ruled by kings and noblemen, but by freedom, equality and fraternity, by *liberté, egalité, fraternité* as it is in French.

And these three words had an enormous effect. They roused people, it was as if they had been waiting to hear them — they shouted them, they roared them, they wrote them on their banners. But no one gave much thought to their real meaning and to their true place in life — and so the French Revolution which began with great hopes took a very tragic and terrible course.

The National Assembly, the deputies of the common people, stayed together in defiance of King Louis XVI and made new laws. The new laws still recognized the King, but only as a servant of the will of the people. His own wishes no longer counted.

And of course, they made laws that from now on the Church and the aristocrats had to pay taxes, just like the bourgeois and the peasants. And they made another law that everybody was free to speak or to write what he believed was true.

These laws made by the National Assembly became famous as the Declaration of the Rights of Man. They were received with joy in Paris, in the whole of France, and by freedom-loving people all over the world.

But while the deputies made all these wise and just laws, the Parisian mob, goaded and incited by rabble-rousers, hunted for men who had made themselves unpopular in the old days: aristocrats who had ill-treated their servants, tax-collectors who had been too harsh, and when they found them they hanged them on lamp-posts in the streets.

And in the countryside bands of peasants burnt down the mansions and castles and murdered noblemen and their families — they even killed servants who remained loyal to their masters.

The aristocrats who could escape were fortunate. Disguised as common people they fled to Italy, Germany and England; many of the courtiers of Louis XVI fled, including his two brothers.

But neither the wise laws of the National Assembly nor the riots of the peasants were any help against the food-shortage. By October of this fateful year 1789, the people of Paris were famished. Once again rumours started, blaming the King for the food-shortage. The starving rabble of the slums, armed with pikes and knives and muskets marched to Versailles. During the day they only shouted and screamed outside the Palace, but when darkness fell they stormed inside. The Queen, Marie Antoinette, just got out of her room in time before the invaders broke in and slashed her bed with cutlasses believing she was still in it.

In the end the mob was driven out of the palace by the National Guard, a kind of police force commanded by Lafayette, the hero of the American War of Independence, who was very popular.

But the mob did not go away. They demanded now that the King and the whole royal family should come with them back to Paris to see for himself how the people suffered.

In order to avoid bloodshed, the King agreed. So he and his wife and children were put in a coach and surrounded by the rabble they left Versailles; they were never to see it again.

On they way the procession met carts taking flour to Paris — which put the mob in a happy mood. They shouted "We bring the baker and his wife to Paris!"

And so Louis XVI came to the old gloomy palace in Paris, the Tuileries, that had stood empty since Louis XIV had built Versailles. A few days later, the National Assembly, too, moved to Paris.

The next events of the French Revolution took place in Paris.

27. The Tuileries

When the National Assembly, the parliament of France, moved to Paris, it became divided into two parties. One party, the Republicans, wanted France to become a republic — like the United States — without king or queen. The other party thought it would be better for France if the King remained, but only as a servant of the will of the people — which is, more or less, as it is in Britain.

As long as there were many deputies who wanted France to be a monarchy, the life of the King was not in danger. There was only one thing that could endanger the King's life: if he tried to flee from France.

Some aristocrats who had escaped to Germany and Austria were busy in forming a small army to invade France; but this was not a very serious threat. However, Leopold II, the Emperor of Austria and brother of Marie Antoinette, was also gathering an army to invade France and rescue his sister, and Frederick William II, the King of Prussia, also was getting troops ready for an invasion of France. The kings and aristocracy in other countries were badly shaken by what happened in France and they wanted to crush the French Revolution before its ideas spread to their own countries. Powerful enemies were getting ready to attack France, and if Louis XVI tried to flee to join these enemies of France, he would be seen as a traitor, as a man who was on the side of Austria and Prussia against his own people.

That is why the deputies who wanted France to be a monarchy warned the King not to make any attempt to escape. If he tried and was caught his life would no longer be safe and even the deputies who were for him would then become his enemies.

Louis XVI was warned repeatedly not to try to flee. It was good advice, but Louis was not a clever man and when some courtiers who still remained with him, told him they had arranged an escape for him and his family, he agreed.

And so, at midnight on July 20, 1791, the royal family crept out of the Tuileries and, set out in a coach drawn by six horses. Through the night and into the next day the coach travelled through France, nearer and nearer to the frontier.

About midday the coach passed through a little village and a young man named Dronet saw the faces of the passengers as the coach rolled by. The young man had some years before been a soldier in Paris, and had seen King Louis XVI, and now recognized his face in the coach. He immediately mounted a horse and, taking a short-cut through the woods, reached the next village where the mayor took quick action. The road was blocked with farm-carts piled together and when the coach came it had to stop. The coach was surrounded by peasants armed with pitchforks and the royal passengers had to get out and were kept as prisoners in the village until Government troops arrived and took them on the sad return-journey to Paris.

The story of this unsuccessful escape shows that the people of France no longer had any love for the King. And as the story of the escape became known, the Frenchmen turned against the King with hatred. They regarded him as a traitor who had tried to join the enemies of France.

One day a mob of twenty thousand — roused and maddened by agitators — broke into the gardens outside the Tuileries in Paris. The guards in the gardens did not know what to do and instead of driving the rabble out, let them rush on, through the gardens and into the palace.

But in the palace the mob faced a different kind of guard, the King's personal Swiss body-guard. These were hand-picked men, Swiss mercenaries who had sworn a solemn oath to defend the royal family. This Swiss body-guard drew their swords, ready to fight the invaders, but at that moment the King appeared, "Put back your swords," he said, "I have nothing to fear from Frenchmen."

Faced with the calm dignity of the King, the ruffians who had stormed in, felt ill at ease. They all wore red caps which were the sign of all fierce republicans. One of the ruffians held out his red cap to the King and the King put it on his own head — whereupon the men cheered. They asked that the Queen and her little son should also put on these "freedom-caps" — and when this was done, they left the palace and persuaded the mob outside to go home. The calmness and dignity of King Louis had prevented a battle between his guards and the mob.

A young officer of the French army had watched with a friend when the mob stormed into the palace-gardens. And this young officer said; "You know, one cannon-shot would have made this crowd run." The name of the young officer was Napoleon Bonaparte; he was one day to become master of France — a master who would not worry about bloodshed as Louis XVI worried.

This invasion of the royal palace by the mob came as a great shock to people outside France. Was it possible that a king should be treated in this fashion?

A Prussian prince, the Duke of Brunswick, was so enraged that he sent a message to France: "If there should be any more acts of violence against king or queen, the armies of Austria and Prussia will come and make the people of France pay with their blood for the insults against royalty." If the noble Duke expected that his message would frighten the French, he was mistaken. All Frenchmen, even those who were friendly to the king and queen — felt that this was an insult to the honour of France. Did these foreigners think France was afraid of them? There was only one way to show them France was not afraid of Prussia or Austria — that was to declare war on them.

And so, France did not wait for Austria or Prussia to invade her, but declared war against them.

But for the mob of Paris, the King and Queen were to blame for the war, it was their friends, — the Emperor of Austria, the King of Prussia, the Duke of Brunswick — who had forced the war on France.

Once again the mob marched to the Tuileries, shouting for the blood of the King and Queen. This time the King was warned in time that he and his family were no longer safe in the palace, that the mob would kill without mercy. Where could he go? The only place which the ruffians would respect was the National Assembly, their parliament. And so the royal family secretly made their way to the National Assembly.

The faithful Swiss guards had not been told that the King and Queen had left, and when the mob came shouting and screaming through the palace gardens, the Swiss opened fire, and that stopped the crowd.

But when the King — who was already under the protection of the National Assembly — heard that his body-guard had fired on Frenchmen, he was horrified. He sent a message to the Swiss soldiers that they were not to fight.

The Swiss had sworn to obey the King, and loyal to their oath they stopped shooting and they sheathed their swords. But for the mob this was like a signal to renew their attack, they stormed into the palace and they killed every Swiss guard. They died — obedient to their oath — without defending themselves. And the invaders rushed into the palace trampling over their bodies, looting and plundering and drinking themselves senseless with wine they found in the cellars.

If the King and Queen thought they were safe in the National Assembly, they were mistaken. In the National Assembly the enemies of the King, the Republicans now had the upper hand. They passed a law which ended the monarchy, declared France a republic and the royal family was arrested and put in a gloomy prison called "The Temple" because it had once been a castle of the Knight Templars.

It was a King of France who had once caused the downfall of the Knight Templars, it was now a castle of the Knight Templars that saw the downfall of the last King of France.

28. Danton, Robespierre and Marat

In 1792 France had answered the threats of the Duke of Brunswick by declaring war on Prussia and Austria. But Prussia and Austria had long prepared for this war, they had an army of eighty thousand trained soldiers ready, as well as a twenty-thousand strong army of the French noblemen and their followers who had escaped from France and hoped to regain their possessions and privileges. This great army now invaded France, led by the sworn enemy of the French Revolution, the Duke of Brunswick.

And France — who started the war — was not at all prepared for it. There was only a small number of trained officers and men and they could not hope to hold up the avalanche of enemy troops now rolling into France.

At that moment — when it seemed that France had lost the war before it even started, when the deputies of the National Assembly who so light-heartedly declared war, trembled with fear — at this moment, one deputy took the lead and saved France. His name was Georges Jacques Danton.

Danton was one of the great orators, a speaker whose words could move the hearts of his listeners. And his fiery speeches put new heart into his fellow-deputies, they roused the national pride of all Frenchmen. Danton called on the French to volunteer for the army, to come and fight for the great ideals — for liberty, equality and fraternity — and the Frenchmen responded to his call. They came in thousands and tens of thousands to fight for France and for these ideals.

In the city of Strasbourg, near the German frontier, a company of French officers sat one night together. In the distance they could hear the rumbling of the Prussian guns. Soon it would be their turn to meet the enemy in battle. But they were not worried, they were cheerful, laughing, joking and drinking.

One of these officers, Rouget de Lisle, was fond of music and had even composed a few songs. One of his friends turned to him saying: "We have heard some pretty songs by you, songs about spring, songs about love, but what we would like tonight is a good marching-song, a song for men who go into battle, a song for men who fight against tyrants, for freedom."

Rouget de Lisle thought for a moment and then replied: "Yes, I think I have the right tune in my mind, and some lyrics also. If you fellows will excuse me, I'll go up to my room and try and put the song on paper."

The hours passed and Rouget sat in his room, trying a few bars on his fiddle, then writing them down by the flickering light of a candle, while the guns rumbled out in the darkness. At sunrise he had his song ready. He sang it to his friends — and there was a storm of applause; yes, this was the kind of song they wanted. And the next day the regiments led by these officers marched into battle with this song on their lips.

Marseille is five hundred miles (800 km) from Strasbourg where the song was composed. Yet, a week later a Marseille newspaper printed the words and the music of this song. The volunteers who joined the army in Marseille liked the song so much that they made it their marching-song.

The volunteers from Marseille were sent to Paris — and as they marched through the city, the people of Paris heard it for the first time. They, too, liked it, sang it and called it "the song from Marseille," the *Marseillaise*. And under that name this stirring song by Rouget de Lisle has remained the French national anthem to this day.

It was this song which inspired the untrained volunteers who had to fight the best-trained soldiers in Europe; it was this song which filled their hearts with courage to fight the foreign invaders.

And the Prussian and Austrian soldiers saw to their amazement that these untrained, poorly armed men — "a rabble" as they call them — marched singing into battle, they marched singing into the most deadly hail of bullets, they stormed strong positions which the Prussians thought could not be taken.

Whole regiments of the French were mown down, but new regiments came to take their place and fight with a contempt for
death, that the trained and drilled soldiers of Prussia and Austria
had never seen before.

The Prussians and Austrians were not cowards — they
fought because they were ordered to fight, they obeyed orders,
but they had no ideas, no beliefs to fight for. However, the
untrained young men of the French army had deep and strong
beliefs. They fought not only for France — but for the ideas that
would enlighten the whole of mankind, for liberty, equality and
fraternity. It was this spirit of the French volunteers — young
men and youngsters of fifteen, sixteen — it was this spirit
which, in the end, proved stronger than the well-drilled armies
of the Prussians and Austrians.

The invaders had come as far as Valmy, only a hundred and
twenty miles from Paris (200 km). But at Valmy, the raw,
untrained recruits of the French inflicted such a crushing defeat
on the well-trained soldiers of the Duke of Brunswick, that the
invaders gave up and retreated hastily to Germany. The battle of
Valmy in 1792 is one of the most important battles in history —
like the battle of Thermopylae, or the battle of Hastings. It was a
battle which showed the world that the spirit of the French
Revolution could not be crushed by force.

But this same year of 1792 in which the Marseillaise was born,
and in which France defeated the invaders at Valmy, also saw
sad and terrible things done in the name of liberty, equality and
fraternity.

When the Prussian and Austrian armies approached Paris,
the fanatical Republicans in the National Assembly decided that
all aristocrats still in France were dangerous, they were only
waiting to help the foreign invaders, so orders were given to kill
them. On four days two thousand people — who had done
nothing wrong — were arrested and shot.

In the same year one of the deputies, Dr Joseph Guillotin,
who thought that the execution of the aristocrats by shooting or
hanging was barbaric and messy, invented a quick and clean
device. He showed his fellow-deputies a little model of his

invention: a broad and heavy knife-blade between two posts, released by a cord. It would cut off a head faster and surer than any axe.

Many deputies laughed when Dr Guillotin said: "This will cut off your head so fast you won't even feel it." Little did these laughing deputies know that many of them would find out for themselves if Dr Guillotin was right. The machine, called *guillotine* was accepted and became the means of execution in France.

The year 1792 was therefore a year of glory and of shame for France — the glory of Valmy and the shame of the murder of the aristocrats. The next year, 1793, could only be called the year of madness.

The fierce, fanatical republicans gained the upper hand in the National Assembly; they called themselves "Jacobins" because the party headquarters used to be a church-hall, belonging to the Church of St Jacques. But, as you will see, these fanatical republicans, the Jacobins, cared little for churches, or religion or saints.

The leaders of this fanatical party were three men. One of them was Danton, the eloquent speaker who roused the pride and patriotism of the French to fight the foreign invaders. Danton was a veritable mountain of a man, enormously tall as well as fat, with a voice like thunder. But if you saw his large, red face, and his great paunch, you knew that this was a man who enjoyed the pleasures of life, food and drink. If Danton had lived 150 years earlier in England he would have fitted well amongst the Cavaliers!

The second leader of the Jacobins was Maximilien Robespierre. He was the very opposite of Danton: a little man, thin, his face so pale it was almost green. He spoke with a dry rasping voice, but his mind was the most cunning in France. This pale, clever little man had no weaknesses like Danton; he never drank anything but water, and only ate the simplest food, and very little of it. Robespierre would have made an excellent Puritan — but an utterly heartless Puritan; Robespierre was a man who never loved anybody or anything in his life.

The third Jacobin leader was Jean-Paul Marat — who was a

gifted but completely dishonest journalist. Marat was one of the first men who discovered that a newspaper has the power to influence the minds of people. A newspaper can make and shape the opinions of people — and they don't even notice that their so-called "own opinions" are only what a newspaper has put into their minds. Marat called his newspaper *L'Ami du People* (The People's Friend); it was a very popular newspaper and the mob of Paris swallowed every lie Marat printed, every distortion and exaggeration, as gospel truth.

These three men, Danton, Robespierre and Marat, the leaders of the Jacobins, held the fate of France in their hands, in that year of madness, 1793.

29. The Reign of Terror

Each of the three men, Danton, Robespierre, Marat, the leaders of the Jacobins, the masters of France in the year of madness, 1793, was really a caricature, a distortion, of one of the great ideals of the Revolution. Danton used his eloquence to play upon the peoples' love of freedom; Robespierre used or rather misused peoples' desire for equality for his own purpose; and Marat, the "friend of the people," appealed through his writing to peoples' sense of brotherhood, of unity, but only to rouse men's cruelty.

The first step in this distortion of *liberté, egalité, fraternité* was the disposal of the King, Louis XVI. Danton, Robespierre and Marat demanded the death of the King as a traitor to France and they received a majority of 53 (387 for, 334 against) in the National Assembly for the execution of the King.

On January 20, 1793, fifteen thousand soldiers lined the streets through which the *tumbril,* the two-wheeled cart, with the King rolled to the great square where the guillotine was waiting. The entire population of Paris was in the streets; windows and even roof-tops were crowded with people.

Louis XVI was, perhaps, too simple-minded for his task as King, but he never lacked courage and he remained calm and fearless to the last. He mounted the wooden steps of the guillotine firmly. Before he put his head under the great knife he wanted to say some final words to the people but — as happened at the execution of Charles I in England — the soldiers beat their drums to drown his voice.

And then the King knelt down, laid his head under the knife, the knife dropped, the head fell into a basket, and the executioner — Sanson by name, held up the head and shouted *"Vive la République"* And *"Vive la République"* the people shouted, throwing their red caps into the air, dancing and singing round the guillotine to the tune of a new popular song: *Ça ira* — "This will go."

Louis was not a bad king — but he paid with his life for the conceit and the stupidity of the kings before him — Louis XV, Louis XIV, right back to Catherine de Medici — who thought she could preserve the royal power by the Massacre of St Bartholomew's Night.

Louis XVI was executed in January 1793. In October Queen Marie Antoinette suffered the same fate. She was only 37 years old but her once golden hair was snow-white when she was led to her death.

Her son was given to a Jacobin shoemaker, who treated the little boy so badly — he starved him and beat him up — that, after two years of suffering, the poor child died.

And in the same year in which the King and Queen were executed, the National Assembly, dominated by Danton, Robespierre, and Marat, passed one law after another, laws which can only be called mad.

One law abolished the calendar counting of years from the birth of Christ. The years should be counted from the birth of the French Republic, 1792. So 1793 became the year 1, 1794 the year two, and so on. Each year was divided into ten months of 36 days, not twelve months any longer.

Then religion was abolished altogether. All churches and monasteries were first plundered and then closed. Instead of the Christian religion the people should worship "Reason." At a great ceremony in Paris, a pretty actress, dressed up in Roman clothes, was shown to the people as Goddess of Reason. It was a cold day and the poor "goddess" fell ill with pneumonia the next day.

All titles, baron, duke, lord — were abolished, even the polite *Monsieur* and *Madame* was no longer allowed. People had to call each other *Citoyen* and *Citoyenne* (citizen).

To wipe out even the memory of royalty, the bodies of the former kings and queens of France were taken from their tombs and thrown into quicklime so that nothing was left of them. Even playing cards had to be changed. Instead of kings, queens, knaves, there were now pictures of ladies supposed to represent liberty, equality, fraternity.

The rest of the world was shocked by the executions and by

these mad laws. Britain, Austria, Spain, Italy, declared war against France. And in France itself whole provinces, cities like Lyons and Toulon rose in rebellion against the mad fanatics in Paris.

France was threatened by powerful enemies outside and by rebellions inside. In this desperate situation, the leaders, Danton, Robespierre, Marat, decide that the first task is to crush their enemies inside France. Marat wrote in his newspaper: "two hundred thousand enemies are in our midst — they must die. Two hundred thousand heads must roll to save the Republic."

In the city of Caen, in Normandy, a young girl, Charlotte Corday read Marat's newspaper every day. She was a Republican with all her heart, she believed wholeheartedly in the great ideals of freedom, equality and brotherhood — but she felt that to demand the death of two hundred thousand fellow-Frenchmen was wrong, was evil. She felt that this man, Marat, was a bloodthirsty monster who must not be allowed to sway the minds of the French people.

And this young, beautiful girl who could easily have lived a happy life in her little town in Normandy, came to a terrible decision: that it was her task to rid France of this monster, Marat.

Charlotte Corday planned the deed carefully. She was known as a fervent Republican and so Marat was not surprised when he received a letter from her in which she said she had discovered a conspiracy against the government and was coming to Paris to give him a list of the wicked plotters. Having written this letter, Charlotte Corday set out for Paris.

Now Marat suffered from an unpleasant skin-disease and the only way in which he could find relief from the itching red spots on his body was in a hot bath. As people had no bath-rooms in those days, Marat kept a small bath-tub — just large enough to sit in — in his bedroom. He used to sit for hours in this little tub and even wrote his newspaper articles sitting in the bath.

When Charlotte Corday arrived, the doorkeeper would not let her in: he told her Marat was in his bath. But the girl said:

"Tell him that Charlotte Corday wants to see him. It is urgent. The safety of France is at stake."

When Marat heard who the visitor was, he remembered her letter and said: "Well, if she does not mind seeing me in my bath, let her come in."

When she entered, Marat peered at her through wisps of steam, rising from his bath. "Well," he said, "let us have the names of the traitors you have discovered."

Charlotte Corday began to dictate a list of names and while Marat was writing them down, she drew a knife from her dress and suddenly stepped forwards and plunged it into his breast. He gave one outcry and died. The cry brought people from outside, and Charlotte Corday was held and taken to prison.

At her trial she said, "I killed Marat because men of his kind are the true enemies of freedom." And she calmly went to the guillotine.

The assassination of Marat frightened and infuriated the Jacobin leaders, Danton and Robespierre. Danton held speeches in which he roared: "Death to all aristocrats, death to anyone who shows by a single word he is not wholeheartedly Republican!" And Robespierre would speak in his monotonous, rasping voice for two hours of the duties of a good citizen, and then end by reading a list of a few hundred names: people who were not good citizens and who therefore, much to his regret, had to be sentenced to death.

The time from 1793 to 1794 is called the "Reign of Terror," the time when Marat's wish was fulfilled and hundreds of thousands of heads rolled.

First all the remaining aristocrats were killed — even those who were Republicans and Jacobins — it was enough that they had been born with a title.

Then came the people who had expressed sympathy or pity for the King; they too had to die. A wrong word could cost a man his life.

A soldier who got drunk and shouted: "France is a great country whether she is a republic or a monarchy," was arrested and his head rolled.

Then came all the deputies who had once voted against the

death-sentence for Louis XVI. Faithful republicans though they were, they had shown sympathy for the King, and now they had to die. They went to their death singing the Marseillaise.

And the priests, monks and nuns of the closed churches and monasteries, were seen as enemies of the Republic. They, too, were led to the guillotine.

By then Danton, the great Danton, became sick of the bloodshed. He appealed to his fellow-deputies to stop the executions. But Robespierre had been waiting for this. He accused Danton and his friends of being traitors, and Danton was sentenced to death and his head rolled.

Now Robespierre, the Puritan, was master of France. He was a great believer in equality. To have better brains than other people was a crime against equality — and so the best minds of France had to die, including a world-famous scientist, Lavoisier. By now his own friends and supporters feared for their lives. So they sprang a surprise on Robespierre and accused him of being a traitor. They had him arrested and sent to the guillotine. People spat at him on his way to his death in 1794. With the death of Robespierre the "Reign of Terror" came to an end. A group of moderates, called the "Directorate" took over the Government of France.

30. Napoleon

Robespierre was certainly a heartless monster, but in his own crazy way he had been sincere in his belief that he was doing his best for France. He himself was convinced that he was a selfless servant of France. The men who had brought about his downfall — a lawyer named Paul Barras and his friends — were not in any sense selfless. They had only stopped the "Reign of Terror" because they feared for their own lives, and once they were in power and installed as the "Directorate," they used their position to make themselves rich.

And things looked quite promising for these "directors" of France. The rebellions in the provinces, in Lyons, in Toulon, had been crushed by the French army, killing many thousands of rebels, so the directors had no fear of any more upheavals in the provinces. In Paris they had disposed of Robespierre and also of a number of other fanatical Jacobins, so they need not fear any enemies from this quarter. And the outside enemies — Britain, Italy, Austria — were in no hurry to invade France, with the Battle of Valmy fresh in their minds.

All seemed good for Barras and his fellow-directors; good, that was, for the pleasant task of amassing a fortune. But things did not work out so well. The year 1795 again brought a poor harvest and a long, hard winter; food became scarce and the price of flour increased, and the poor could no longer pay for bread. And then the people of Paris did what they had done before — they rioted.

But the "directors" of France were not going to allow any riots in Paris. And Barras and his friends thought of a very capable young general who had already shown that he could deal with rebellious crowds: he had crushed the rebellion in Toulon. And so Barras sent for this promising young general and gave him the task of disbanding the mob. The name of this young general was Napoleon Bonaparte.

General Bonaparte brought peace and order to Paris in his own way. His troops marched at night into Paris and surrounded the gardens of the Tuileries with forty cannons.

Next morning the rioters were out again, streaming from the poor suburbs of Paris to the centre, to the Tuileries, crowding the gardens and shouting: "Bread, bread, give us bread!" When the yelling crowd approached the soldiers General Bonaparte shouted a warning to the people in front. But they only laughed. Who would dare shoot at the people of Paris? And in any case they were not going to take orders from this little man, so they came nearer. When they advanced further, Bonaparte shouted "Fire." The cannons wreaked havoc on the packed mass of people; hundreds were killed by one volley and the rest fled in terror.

General Bonaparte was the same man who, as an officer, had seen the mob invade the Tuileries and who had said to a friend: "One cannon-shot would make them run." He had remembered his words and had acted accordingly. And that was how he brought order to Paris.

Barras and his fellow-directors thanked General Bonaparte, but thought it would be wise to get this ruthless and ambitious young man away from Paris and away from France. So they put him in command of the French troops that had invaded Italy, and it was in Italy that Bonaparte first proved himself as one of the greatest generals in history.

Napoleon Bonaparte was born on the island of Corsica in the Mediterranean. The people of Corsica are actually Italian and their language is an Italian dialect, but France had bought the island from Italy and so Corsica had come under the rule of France. Napoleon was born on this island in 1769, when Louis XV and Madame de Pompadour were still ruling France. The Bonaparte family was large — Napoleon had four brothers and three sisters. The father, a lawyer, was only too glad when the French Governor of Corsica offered a "scholarship" for one of his sons — he would be given a free education at a military academy in France where boys were educated and trained to become officers in the French army. The father was relieved to not have to worry about the education of one of his eight children, and so young Napoleon was sent to this boarding school, the Military Academy.

Napoleon had a tough time at this school. The other boys teased him because he spoke French with an Italian accent and he made no friends amongst them. But this pale boy from Corsica did not seem to need any friends, he seemed quite content to be alone with his thoughts, and, through time the other boys learned to respect him. When there was snow, the boys used to split up into two teams fighting each other with snowballs. But the team in which this Corsican boy always ended up, took him as their commander and leader — even older boys simply accepted him as leader — and his team always won.

Napoleon Bonaparte finished school and became a lieutenant. But even as an officer he had no close friends. The other officers came from noble and rich families and had plenty of money from home besides their army-pay. Bonaparte only had his army-pay which was not much and the young aristocrats tended to look down on the lieutenant because he was not of their own class. But Napoleon Bonaparte was reading the books of enlightenment; he read about the natural rights of man, he heard of the great ideas of freedom, equality and brotherhood and he dreamed of a time when a man's own ability rather than privileges of birth would decide his career in life. And he was sure of his own abilities — he was sure he was destined for greatness.

When the Revolution came, Lieutenant Bonaparte was not interested in the fate of the unhappy King Louis XVI, he was not interested in the Republican Government — in men like Danton, Robespierre, Marat — for Bonaparte realized that these men were only distorting the ideals of liberty, equality and fraternity. But, at least, this Republican Government did away with the old privileges and this would give him a chance for advancement, for promotion which the old regime would not have given him. That is why Bonaparte served the Republican Government faithfully, and bombarded the rebels of Toulon.

As a reward he had a rapid promotion and was already a general when Barras called him to Paris to quell the riots. For General Bonaparte this was only another step on the ladder to greatness and fame and, as you have heard, he quelled the riots with one shot from his cannons. His reward was to be given command of the troops fighting in Italy.

By that time Napoleon had married an attractive widow, Josephine Beauharnais. And when he left his wife he said: "My sword is at my side and with it I shall go far."

In the year 1795, France was at war with Britain, Prussia, Austria, Spain, Italy. What chance did she have to win against all these enemies? None at all — had it not been for this man from Corsica, Napoleon Bonaparte.

The French troops in Italy were poorly equipped, badly clothed and in poor spirit. But with his mere presence Bonaparte created a new spirit amongst them. They initially defeated an Italian army — and then came up against a great army the Austrians had sent into Italy. The battle against the Austrians took place in November 1796, near a village called Arcole in northern Italy.

The Austrians were on the other side of the River Alpone and the French could only get at them by crossing a bridge. But the Austrians had trained their cannons on the bridge and every time the French came upon the bridge they were mown down by the Austrian guns.

Three times the French advanced on the bridge — and then retreated under a hail of fire from the Austrians, leaving their dead and wounded behind. Then General Bonaparte himself took the French flag, and shouting "Follow me," ran onto the bridge, and his faithful soldiers followed him. They reached the middle of the bridge, but now the cannon fire was so heavy that the soldiers turned back. In the confusion Bonaparte fell from the bridge into the mud and swamp below and Austrian soldiers came running towards him. The French soldiers saw it, and with the shout, "Forward, save the General!" they stormed across the bridge, drove the Austrians away and, at the end of the day, had gained a decisive victory.

Within a short time the whole of Italy was in the hands of General Bonaparte and the people of Paris received him in triumph. The shooting in the Tuileries Gardens was forgotten — he was their beloved hero.

31. Egypt

Napoleon Bonaparte was not tall; he was short and stout and his soldiers used to speak of him affectionately as "our little corporal." But in this little, stout man there lived an iron will, a drive and energy which made all the taller people feel dwarfed in his presence.

And this little man was, indeed, a giant in his mental capacities. He was, first of all, a giant for work — he could dictate five letters at the same time. For most part of his life he never slept more than three hours a day. The planning and preparing of battles and whole campaigns, the discussions with his officers, the inspections of troops, these were only a part of his work. When he had conquered a region he laid down the rules of government, the laws for this region and these rules and laws were in the spirit of the French Revolution: equality of justice, equal opportunities for all.

He was not only a giant in the amount of work he got done in a day, he was also a giant in his plans for the future. His great dream, his great ambition was to unite all the nations of Europe in one great nation. He wanted to do away with the dozens of nationalities and kingdoms of Europe which were for ever bickering and warring amongst themselves. But as they showed no inclination to join together of their own free will, they should be *made* to come together — and he was the man to make them into one nation.

He was also a giant in the way he impressed people. From his pale face there blazed a pair of black eyes which had a magnetic power. If he looked at you in anger, you felt as if you were struck by lightning, but if he looked at you with praise and approval you felt your soul lifted with joy.

His soldiers — from the lowest private to the highest officer — not only loved him, they almost worshipped him. He was a kind of god for them. He could demand any hardship, any sacrifice from them and they were happy to serve him, to march for him, to fight for him, and even to die for him.

It may sound quite incredible to us, but on one occasion when he gave a regiment the order to wade into a river and cross to the other side, many men were swept away by the strong current and drowned, but the drowning men cried, "Long live Napoleon," with their last breath.

He was like a higher being, a superhuman being to his soldiers, and even other people in his presence felt as if a more than human force had taken possession of the body of this man and worked through him. It was *not* a truly divine force, like the one that guided humble Joan of Arc, neither was it an evil, devilish force, like the one which drove the monster, Robespierre; it was like a force of nature, a thunderstorm, or a hurricane. It was certainly not like the forces of an ordinary human being.

General Bonaparte's victory in Italy came as a shock and surprise to the enemies of France. Austria quickly asked for peace, and so did Prussia and Spain. Only one country was not shaken and continued the war, and that was Britain. But this was only a war at sea, a war between ships, and was no real danger to France.

For the French people, General Napoleon Bonaparte had with one stroke brought peace and glory to France and he was their beloved hero.

The Directorate, Barras and his fellow-directors, were not very happy about the popularity of General Bonaparte. He was loved by the people, loved by the soldiers, he was ambitious — he might well have ideas about making himself master of France. And so the Directors of France were well pleased when Napoleon Bonaparte himself came to them with a proposal that would take him away from France for a long time.

By this time Britain had established a large colony in Asia — the great subcontinent of India had come under British rule. France did not have enough ships to attack India by sea, but India could also be reached by land. Had Alexander the Great not done that?

What General Bonaparte proposed was this: he would first conquer Egypt, and then he would go on, conquer Turkey and Persia and march through into India and take it from the British.

It was a madly ambitious idea. Even a modern army with tanks and aeroplanes could hardly cope with such a task. But the Directors agreed because it would, at least, keep this dangerous man away from France, a long way away.

And so, in 1798, Napoleon sailed from Toulon with a large fleet, carrying an army of forty thousand soldiers. With this army there came a second little army of scientists, artists, archaeologists. They hoped to make valuable discoveries in the lands of the Orient.

As a matter of fact, at least one great discovery was made on this fantastic expedition. The writing of ancient Egypt, the hieroglyphs, could not be read by anybody in the world. The knowledge of what these pictures meant had completely disappeared. But on this expedition the French scholars discovered a stone in Egypt, the famous Rosetta Stone on which the names of kings and queens was written in Greek letters as well as in hieroglyphs. The discovery of the Rosetta Stone made it possible to decipher all the writing of ancient Egypt. This Rosetta Stone is now in the British Museum in London.

But this important discovery came much later. To begin with, the French fleet with all the soldiers aboard might easily not have reached Egypt at all, because a great British fleet was in the Mediterranean on the look-out for the French and ready to send them to the bottom of the sea. This British fleet was under the command of Horatio Nelson who became the most famous of British sea-heroes.

On this occasion, luck was with Napoleon and his fleet. The British never caught sight of the French ships which landed safely, without meeting any resistance, on the Egyptian coast not far from Alexandria.

At that time Egypt was not an independent country but was under Turkish dominion, as part of the Ottoman Empire. The Turks, however, were completely taken by surprise by the invasion, and so Napoleon not only landed his troops but occupied the city of Alexandria without encountering Turkish soldiers. From Alexandria Napoleon marched his army towards the capital of Egypt, towards Cairo.

They reached Gizah on the outskirts of Cairo, and there they saw the Pyramids and the Sphinx. But there they saw also a great Turkish army rapidly approaching. This was to be the decisive battle for Egypt. Napoleon addressed his soldiers before the battle and in his speech he said, "Soldiers of France, you are going to fight in front of the Pyramids. Four thousand years of history look down on you from these monuments. Be worthy of this great occasion." And the Battle of the Pyramids ended with a great French victory.

After this victory Napoleon ordered the ships of his fleet to remain at anchor at a port called Aboukir while he and the army marched on to strike against Turkey. But while they were on the march the British fleet under Nelson — at long last — found the French ships. Nelson sailed his fleet to the port of Aboukir and, in a overnight battle that lasted eighteen hours, the French ships were destroyed and sunk. This event of August 1–2, 1798 became known as the Battle of the Nile.

When the news of the loss of his fleet reached Napoleon he realized that without ships his great plan was doomed. He would need supplies, he would need more troops, and he could not get them without a fleet. He left his army in Egypt and sailed back to France in a little vessel that had been left. And he was once again lucky because this little ship was not caught by the British and arrived safely in France.

The poor soldiers left behind in Egypt, were later defeated by the British, taken prisoner and, eventually, sent back to France. The British had spoiled Napoleon's great plan to imitate Alexander the Great. It was Nelson who had spoiled it. The Rosetta Stone, that the French had discovered, was part of the booty the British took from the French troops in Egypt, and that is why the stone is not in Paris but in London.

You might think the French people gave Napoleon a poor welcome after the disaster of this expedition. Far from it; they cheered him as if he had conquered India, and they were pleased to have him back. In his absence Austria had again declared war on France, and the war was going badly for the French. Napoleon Bonaparte was the only man who could turn defeat into victory.

32. Emperor Napoleon and Trafalgar

The French people welcomed Napoleon on his return from Egypt because they hoped he would save them from the Austrian armies. But there was also another reason. The Directorate, Barras and his friends, had never been very popular and their policy of using government mainly to make themselves rich had not endeared them to the people. Many in France said quite openly they would sooner be ruled by Bonaparte than by these men who only wanted to fill their own pockets. In addition the Army, the French soldiers, admired Napoleon and despised the Directors.

Bonaparte himself was always keenly aware of public opinion, and as things were going in his favour, he was not a man to miss an opportunity. One day in November 1799, he strode into a meeting of the French deputies (Members of Parliament), told them that the Directorate was finished and that he would take over the government under the title "First Consul" — a title the ancient Romans had used when Rome was still a republic.

The deputies objected; they shouted at him; they called him a "dictator." Napoleon walked out of the hall where a company of his soldiers was waiting. "Send this rabble away!" he said. And with the cry, "Long live Napoleon," the soldiers stormed in and a few minutes later the hall was cleared. France had a new government: the Consul Napoleon Bonaparte.

The first task of the new Consul was to deal with the Austrian threat. After the Battle of Arcole (when he stormed over the bridge) Napoleon had conquered Italy. But while he was away in Egypt, the Austrians had reoccupied Northern Italy so he had to drive them out again. However, by this time it was January, deep winter, and no general in his senses would move an army through ice and snow., at least that's what the Austrians thought; they expected Napoleon to come and attack them in spring.

But Napoleon had different ideas — he remembered a great general who had once invaded Italy from the north, by coming over the Alps: Hannibal. Napoleon was going to do what Hannibal had done; he had no elephants, but he did cross the Alps with his army in the depth of winter.

The army had heavy cannons which had to be pulled up steep slopes, but the soldiers made great sledges of pinewood and on these sledges they heaved and pulled the guns up through the deep snow. At some places there was not even a path, only a ledge so narrow that a false step, a slip in the snow would send a man crashing down to his death. Yet, along the narrow ledges and clinging to cliffs the soldiers toiled and pulled, and when they felt exhausted and at the end of their strength, they only had to see their general to feel new courage and strength.

At long last they reached the famous St Bernard Monastery at the highest point of the St Bernard Pass. The monks could hardly believe their eyes when they saw a whole army coming up at a time when, normally, not a single traveller came that way.

The way down the pass was just as dangerous, now the trouble was to stop the sledges with the guns from running away and from crashing into the men in front.

Somehow they made it, they crossed the Alps and poured into Northern Italy. The Austrians, taken by surprise, lost battle after battle and after a crushing defeat at Marengo in 1800, came begging for peace. Not only Austria but Britain too made peace with France. Imagine the joy and jubilation in Paris, and in the whole of France. Napoleon Bonaparte, the First Consul, had indeed worked a miracle and no praise was too high for him, the victorious hero of France.

The time had come for Napoleon to aim even higher. Why should he remain First Consul when he could have a crown? But he was not to be a mere *King* — he was going to be *Emperor* of France, as Charlemagne had been. He always had great examples from history to inspire him: Alexander the Great, Hannibal, now it was Charlemagne.

Amidst pomp and splendour the day came when Napoleon
Bonaparte, the son of a Corsican lawyer, and his wife, Josephine,
were crowned Emperor and Empress of France. And no one less
than the Pope had to come from Rome to hand the imperial
crown to Napoleon at the coronation. But it was Napoleon who
put the crown on his own head as well as crowning his wife,
Josephine. This was to show that, unlike Charlemagne, he owed
the crown to himself and not to the Pope. Napoleon Bonaparte
had become the Emperor Napoleon, but he knew that it was the
French Revolution which had opened the way to the throne for
him — it was his own ability *and* the French Revolution which
had carried him so high, and not the blessing of the Pope.

For Napoleon to be Emperor of France was only the beginning. He said: "There will be no peace in Europe until it is
united under one government." There was no doubt which
government he had in mind: his own.

It is not surprising that the other nations of Europe were
worried, so the three main powers in Europe at that time,
Britain, Austria and Russia formed an alliance. If one of these
countries was attacked by Napoleon, the other two would come
to its aid.

Napoleon did not like that at all — and he disliked Britain
most. He called the British contemptuously "a nation of shop-
keepers" and he, a born soldier, could only despise businessmen. But these "shop-keepers" had spoiled his plans in Egypt,
they had formed an alliance against him, it was high time that he
taught them a lesson.

He would invade England — and, indeed, French troops
were massed along the Channel and people in England expected
an invasion at any moment. But Napoleon was not such a fool
as to attempt an invasion as long as there was a British navy that
could send his invading ships to the bottom of the sea. First the
British Navy had to be destroyed.

Napoleon therefore ordered his Admiral Villeneuve to draw
the British fleet away from the Channel and to destroy it on the
high seas.

The French admiral fulfilled the first part of this order —
and so it came that the French fleet and the British fleet came to

grips with each other not in the Channel but in Spanish waters, off Cape Trafalgar.

The commander of the British fleet was once again Admiral Nelson. It is strange to think that this great sailor was sea-sick every time he put to sea. And he had lost his right eye and his right arm in sea-battles. This one-eyed, sea-sick disabled individual was the man who saved Britain from invasion.

On October 21, 1805 Nelson, standing on the deck of his flagship *Victory,* watched the approaching French fleet. On his orders signal-flags were run up on the mast of the *Victory,* it was a signal that has become famous in history: "England expects every man to do his duty." And from all the ships a mighty cheer went up as the sailors read the signal.

As the two fleets came closer the guns began to roar — and then the *Victory* went into action. The French poured shot after shot into Nelson's ship, but the *Victory* closed in on a French ship. Then there came a shot from high up in the rigging of the Frenchman, and Nelson was hit in the shoulder. He fell down and whispered to Hardy, the captain of the *Victory,* "They have done for me this time, Hardy." But, lying on the deck, Nelson put a handkerchief over his wound, he did not want the sailors to see that he had received a fatal wound.

One hour later Nelson was still alive and he heard his sailors cheer. And then Captain Hardy bent down to him: "Ten French ships have been sunk, fifteen have surrendered, they are finished." "Thank God," said Nelson. "I have done my duty." And with these words he died.

The Battle of Trafalgar is — after the Armada — the most important sea-battle in British history. It saved Britain from the invasion by Napoleon's troops. With his own fleet destroyed and the British fleet in command of the Channel Napoleon had to give up his plans of invasion. Twice — at Aboukir and at Trafalgar — it was Nelson who had frustrated Napoleon's plans.

33. Austerlitz. Wellington. Russia 1812

Napoleon wanted a "united Europe" — though he was far ahead of his time in his wish — but he wanted to unite the nations of Europe by *force* and under his own rulership; and so the idea of a united Europe — good as it may have been — brought war and suffering and bloodshed.

Napoleon had failed to conquer Britain, he had failed through the valour of Nelson and his sailors, but on land he did defeat the armies of Britain, Austria and Russia.

At Austerlitz the combined Austrian and Russian armies far outnumbered the French, but Napoleon was so certain of victory that he said to his generals on the morning of the battle: "Look at that red sunrise, this is the sun that will see my great victory." And so it was. The Russian and Austrian armies were not only defeated but destroyed in this Battle of Austerlitz in 1805.

After this crushing defeat Austria gave up the struggle — and there was no longer any country on the Continent to oppose Napoleon except perhaps Russia, but even Russia could no longer interfere with his plans. With that in mind, Napoleon set about remaking Europe according to his own ideas.

He took Northern Italy (which had been part of the Austrian Empire) for himself and assumed the title "King of Italy." But in Southern Italy he formed a new kingdom, the Kingdom of Naples which he gave to one of his generals, Murat, who became King of Naples.

Another general, Bernadotte, was given Sweden and became King of Sweden. As it happened, in all the upheavals that came later, Bernadotte (who was originally a cook) remained King of Sweden and the present King of Sweden is a descendant of Napoleon's general, Bernadotte.

In addition to his generals, Napoleon also had brothers to reward. One brother was given Holland, becoming King of Holland. Another brother was given a slice of Germany called Westphalia, and a third was made King of Spain.

So, Napoleon — now at the pinnacle of his power — looked after his generals and after his brothers well. His old mother, Lactitia Bonaparte, was given a luxurious home in Paris, but the old Corsican woman kept on grumbling and mumbling, "I wonder how long all this is going to last."

Napoleon had no such worries: he was going to make it last. His main concern was to have a son who could inherit this great empire. Unfortunately, his wife, the Empress Josephine, had not given him any children — it seems she could not have any — and so Napoleon divorced her. He had to have a son. Who was to be his second wife? His choice fell on a princess of the noblest blood in Europe: the daughter of the Emperor of Austria. Neither the Emperor, nor the princess could refuse the most powerful man in Europe. And so Napoleon — who had once approved when another Austrian princess, Marie Antoinette, went to the guillotine — married Marie Louise, the daughter of the Austrian Emperor. A year later in 1811 a son was born who received the title King of Rome while still in his cradle. Napoleon was certain that his son would inherit an empire as great as the dominions of ancient Rome.

By that time, however, there were already cracks in his empire. One of these cracks was in Spain. Napoleon had made one of his brothers King of Spain and there was a French army in Spain to make sure he remained King. But the Spaniards hated the foreign ruler, they formed little bands, called "guerrillas" (from *guerra,* war) and these guerrilla-bands ambushed and killed a few French soldiers here, a few there. Some guerrillas were caught and shot by the French, but there were always others to carry on the fight.

What made it worse was that the British, these "shopkeepers," had sent an army into Spain through Portugal. The commander of these British troops was a general who was to become famous, the Duke of Wellington, his soldiers called him the "Iron Duke." Wellington did not have an army large enough to drive the French out of Spain, but he could keep them busy; they had to fight continually so Spain was never a safe possession for Napoleon.

Napoleon could have finished Wellington and the guerrillas in Spain if there had been time, but there was no time because a greater army was preparing to strike against him: Russia.

Napoleon knew that Russia was getting ready to declare war against him, and he decided to strike first and invade Russia before the Russian armies were ready.

Russia is a vast country — and for the conquest of Russia Napoleon needed the largest army he had ever commanded. Not only the French, but Prussian, Italian, Austrian regiments had to join to make up the great army — *la grande Armée* as he called it — that was to conquer Russia.

In 1812, *la grande Armée* was ready. Half a million soldiers — the largest army Europe had ever seen up to that time — was on the march and entered Russia. Napoleon expected the Russians to give battle — but they did nothing of the kind. The Russian armies retreated and retreated. But as they withdrew they destroyed crops, they burnt down fields, and villages, they set their own cities on fire. As Napoleon's troops advanced they found nothing but ruins, deserted villages, and fields that were dead and barren, nothing but "scorched earth." Napoleon did not know it yet — but it was this "scorched earth" that was going to defeat him.

All through summer and autumn of 1812 *la grande Armée* kept on trudging over the vast plains of Russia — and the Russians retreated without giving battle but leaving to their enemies only "scorched earth."

In October 1812, Napoleon and his army reached Moscow — and Moscow, too, was deserted and empty, a whole city of empty houses, empty streets, empty and silent. It suited Napoleon, the empty houses would make excellent quarters for his army and give shelter during the terrible cold of the Russian winter.

But the troops had hardly moved in when fires started all over the city, fires laid by the Russians. A few hundred of these Russians were caught and shot, but this did not stop the raging fires and Moscow went up in flames.

Napoleon stared gloomily at the billowing flames and smoke. It was October, the terrible Russian winter was coming, there was no shelter for his half million men. There was only one thing to do: retreat, to get out of this accursed country.

This retreat from Moscow was a disaster: the weather grew colder and colder; the food became scarcer and scarcer; the soldiers grew weaker and weaker.

Snow fell in great, blinding flakes, blizzards howled, the cold seemed to cut to the bone, and thin uniforms were no protection at all. As they stumbled and trudged knee-deep in snow, men fell down from hunger and exhaustion, but no one who could still walk bothered — men threw away their weapons and abandoned their guns.

Then the Russians came. The Cossacks, the Russian horsemen, swooped down on stragglers, killed them and disappeared again. And so the road on which *la grande Armée* stumbled in retreat was strewn with corpses, soon covered with an icy blanket of snow.

Napoleon left his struggling army behind. By changing horses and hardly allowing himself any rest he got out of Russia and back to Paris while his men were still trying to escape from frost, hunger and Russian guns. But only half of *la grande Armée* came back. Two hundred and fifty thousand died in the Russian snows.

The disastrous retreat from Moscow, initiated the downfall of Napoleon. The good fortune which had been with him for so long, now left him.

34. Elba. Waterloo

After the disaster of the Russian campaign, the countries which had bowed so unwillingly to Napoleon's will now rose against him. Prussia and Austria joined with the victorious Russians and turned against Napoleon. They offered him an honourable peace: he could remain Emperor of France but should give up his other conquests. But this was not Napoleon's way — it was "all or nothing" for him, he could never be satisfied with that.

This ultimately led to the "Battle of the Nations" near the German city of Leipzig in 1813. In this battle the French fought against the combined forces of Prussia, Austria and Russia. The battle raged for three days — but Napoleon's star was no longer rising, and he was defeated. He was driven back to France — and, in the end, had to surrender.

The victorious allies forced Napoleon to abdicate, to renounce the throne of France. They did not want another Republican government in France, so a brother of the last King, Louis XVI, who had escaped to England was recalled and became King of France under the name Louis XVIII (Louis XVII was the poor boy who had died under the harsh treatment of the shoemaker).

Napoleon was eventually banished to a little Mediterranean island of Elba between Italy and Corsica.

As a result of the Napoleonic Wars all the old frontiers had been changed so often that it was impossible to go back to things as they had been before. A congress was held in Vienna in which all the nations of Europe were to take part, and in which all claims should be settled fairly and peacefully.

For a whole year the statesmen of Europe debated and argued at this Congress of Vienna, but their discussions were rudely shattered by the news that Napoleon had escaped from Elba and had landed in France.

The new King of France had sent troops against him. They

had orders to shoot him. But Napoleon calmly walked towards the soldiers and cried: "Is there one of you who wants to shoot the Emperor? Here I am!" His old magic worked again: the soldiers shouted, *"Vive l'Empereur!"* and offered to fight for him.

And they came, regiment after regiment, the men who had marched with him in the burning sands of Egypt, who had crossed the snows of the St Bernard Pass with him, who had shared victories in Italy and Austria and Germany with him — they all came to serve him again, to fight for him and to die for him. It seems incredible, but to his soldiers Napoleon was a kind of god.

This new venture of Napoleon's lasted exactly a hundred days. The nations who had bickered and argued at the Congress of Vienna, quickly came to full agreement against the common enemy.

The Duke of Wellington, the Iron Duke, who had fought the French so well in Spain was in command of a British force which was to attack Napoleon from Belgium, and a Prussian army under General Blücher was to join the British from Germany.

Napoleon decided to fight Wellington before the Prussians arrived and attacked the British at Waterloo (in what is now Belgium).

Hour after hour the French stormed against the "square formations" of the British, but Wellington's men held their ground. The fury of the French attack increased, and Wellington began to fear his men could not hold out much longer, but just in the nick of time the Prussians arrived.

With the Prussians on their side, the British went into attack — the French fighting spirit was broken.

Only the soldiers of Napoleon's "Old Guard" stood their ground. They were surrounded on all sides and asked to surrender. They answered proudly: "The Guard can die but it cannot surrender." And they died, fighting to the last man.

This was the famous Battle of Waterloo, June 18, 1815, the last in the Napoleonic Wars.

After his defeat, Napoleon made his way to a port where he gave himself up to the captain of a British ship, the *Bellerophone*.

He became the prisoner of the British Government. It was decided to send him to a place from which he could not escape as he had done from Elba: the little island of St Helena in the South Atlantic — half-way between Africa and South America.

On St Helena Napoleon lived for another six years. He used to go for walks at his own furious pace (he could never walk slowly), or he stood staring over the sea and remembering another island, the island where he was born, Corsica. During that time he wrote his autobiography, the story of his life.

Napoleon had tried to unite Europe in one empire, and he had failed. But — whether he knew it or not — he had carried the ideas of the French Revolution into every country in Europe. The nations of Europe, Prussia, Austria, Russia, they were still ruled by kings and emperors who had absolute power, they still had aristocrats who enjoyed special privileges, but with the French armies the ideas of the French Revolution had arrived. The laws Napoleon had passed, too, had been fairer than the ancient laws of the conquered countries.

And the common people all over Europe were no longer satisfied to live obediently under their rulers and noblemen as they had done before Napoleon, they too demanded a new order of freedom, equality and brotherhood.

So Napoleon, who finished the French Revolution when he made himself Emperor, really carried the spirit of the French Revolution to all nations of Europe.

Yet, think of all the bloodshed which had happened to spread these ideas — the Reign of Terror, the wars of Napoleon. And think of that strange man, the Count of St Germain. If Louis XV had followed his advice the changes which had to come would not have been so violent, they would have been gradual and the world would have been spared much suffering.

The Nineteenth and
Twentieth Centuries

35. The Threefold State

The word "body" not only refers to the human body, but can also be used in a different sense. In the legal profession, the word is also used with a quite different meaning. A group of people who act together, and together are responsible, is called "a body" — the social body.

We all, men, women and children, rich and poor, are part of the social body of our country — and, perhaps, even of a larger "social body."

Now such a social body as Britain, or Germany, or France produces all kinds of things: the farmers produce food, the factories produce machines, the writers produce books, the actors produce plays, the government produces laws, and so on.

But there is such a vast difference between the work of an actor or painter and the work of a farmer that one has really to make a division between one kind of work and another.

On one side there is all the work which in one way or another satisfies our physical needs: food, clothes, furniture, cars, and so on. And there is the other work which in one way or another satisfies the mind: books, theatres, films, paintings, music, but also schools and universities, as well as churches or temples, mosques or synagogues. So one part of all the work that is going on is devoted to our physical needs — the factories and farms produce, the shops sell, the railways and lorries transport the goods from place to place — and all this work which gives us the things our bodies need, is called *economy* (from Greek *oikonomos,* the steward, or house-manager).

The other work — in schools and colleges, in the artist's studio, in concert halls and theatres, in the churches, and in newspapers and books, all that work which is for the mind, the spirit, is called *culture.*

In addition there is another kind of work: the Government produces laws, but there is also the police which has to see that the laws are kept, there are judges and lawyers, and there is the army, navy and air-force; all this is the third part of the "social body." All this third part is under the order of the Government, and as Government is elected by political action, it is called *politics* (from Greek *politeia*, citizenship).

Whatever people do to earn a living belongs to one of these three groups, *culture, politics, economy*.

Just as the human physical body is threefold, so the "social" body is threefold, consisting of culture, politics, economy. One could compare culture with the head (which also does not produce anything physical), economy with the limbs, and politics with the rhythmic system.

Now in Europe five hundred, six hundred years ago, all that which I have called "culture" was firmly ruled by the Church. The popes and bishops decided what should be taught in schools and universities, what plays might be performed, what books should be published, and any disobedience was heresy, and could end in torture or death at the stake. Culture was entirely in the hands of the Church.

The other two parts, politics as well as economy were just as firmly under the authority of the king. The king gave laws and his soldiers enforced them. The king gave land to whom he liked, and so controlled the food-production.

But as the modern time approached — from the Renaissance onwards — there came that great change. People were no longer willing to blindly obey the Church or the kings. Of course, neither Church nor kings gave up their powers without a struggle, and so came the wars of religion, the Civil War in England, the Glorious Revolution, and the American Revolution.

In France, the kings and the Church held on to their power longer than in Britain, and the result was the terrible events of the French Revolution.

During the French Revolution the words "Liberty, Equality, Fraternity" sounded for the first time — it was as if people had been waiting to hear these words, they rejoiced in shouting them, they sang them, they put them on flags and coins, on the coat of arms and on statues. Not only in France, but all over the world people thought that with these three words, with these three ideas, a new age of happiness for all would come. But, beautiful as the ideas were, the people who shouted them did not give much thought as to how they should be put into practice. The result was chaos and the guillotine, and in the end the dictator, Napoleon, came to power.

The three words Liberty, Equality, Fraternity can only be meaningful when they are used separately, with reference to each of the three divisions of the social body. Liberty belongs to culture, equality to politics and law, brotherhood to economics. During the French Revolution there was no comprehension of this: Robespierre sent the great scientist Lavoisier to the guillotine simply because he was a better scientist than others and thus sinned against equality. Marat told people to form a brotherhood for the purpose of killing aristocrats; it was chaos. Even in the time after the French Revolution, after Napoleon, the three ideas were still rather like dynamite — if people handled them wrongly the result was upheaval and bloodshed.

At the time of the French Revolution, while all this noise and fighting was going on, there was also another great change. This change came so silently that no one realized at the time that it was a far more important change than the French Revolution and the Napoleonic Wars. This silent revolution changed life completely; it brought great blessings and also terrible misery.

But this silent revolution made the three ideals, Liberty, Equality Fraternity even more urgent, more necessary than they were before, yet hardly anyone at the time realized it.

36. The Beginning of the Industrial Revolution

The silent revolution, the Industrial Revolution began in England, in Lancashire in the year 1764. By that time the making of woollen and cotton cloth had become a great industry in Lancashire. However, there were no factories, no smoking chimneys, only small towns and villages. The two processes involved in making cloth, the spinning and the weaving, were done in people's homes.

Usually it was the father of the family who sat at the weaving loom and sent the "shuttle" backwards and forwards. The wife and children did the spinning of the yarn using a spinning wheel. A pedal turned a large wheel which drove a little spindle much faster. As it rotated, it twisted a thin sliver of wool into a thread.

Now in that year 1764, one Lancashire weaver in the village of Blackburn, James Hargreaves by name, accidentally knocked his wife's spinning wheel over so that it was flat on the ground and the wheel was still turning. His wife, Jenny Hargreaves called him a clumsy lout, but the man paid no attention, he kept on staring at the turning wheel.

"What's the matter with you?" asked Jenny.

"You know," said James Hargreaves, "looking at that thing, it just occurred to me that if one arranged the whole contraption as it is now — horizontally — one could make this one great wheel turn not only one but many spindles, even eight of them. All it needs is to make the wheel drive several transmission bands which turn several spindles."

That was the idea that came to Jimmy Hargreaves as he looked at his wife's spinning wheel on the floor: that by using several transmission bands on the same wheel, several spindles could be turned, which means that turning one wheel, one could make not only one, but several threads at the same time.

Now the Hargreaves were so poor that they did not even have a weaving loom of their own. James Hargreaves and several other equally poor weavers worked for a Mr Peel who owned a number of looms put up in a shed. So when Jenny made her yarn she could not give it to her husband — she had to sell it to Mr Peel who, then, gave it to the weavers. As you can imagine these weavers who worked only for a wage were much worse off than a weaver who owned his own loom and could sell the cloth he made. Hargreaves was one of the poor weavers who did not possess their own looms — and all he thought was: if Jenny can twist eight threads with one turn of the wheel she will make eight times more yarn per day than before — and that will bring us eight times more money.

And so with a few carpenters' tools Hargreaves set about changing Jenny's spinning wheel so that it could drive eight spindles. But as he worked and experimented, it occurred to him that this new kind of spinning wheel should be kept secret. If other women all produced eight times more yarn, there would be so much yarn that the price of yarn would go down, and in the end they would produce more yarn but still get as little as before. So Hargreaves wanted his invention to remain a secret.

Hargreaves changed Jenny's spinning wheel and eventually it worked producing eight times more yarn — and every week Jenny took a quantity of yarn to Mr Peel which astonished everybody. How was it possible that this woman could make so much yarn with one wheel? The other women in the village would not leave Jenny in peace, and in a small village where everybody knows everybody else, and where people walk into each other's houses any time of day, in such a village, one can't keep any secrets. Perhaps, Jenny was also proud of her husband's cleverness and blurted out what he had done with her spinning wheel; in any case, the principle: one wheel with several transmission bands to drive more spindles, that principle became known in the village, and all the women demanded that their husbands make them a "spinning jenny" as they called it.

Soon the news spread from Blackburn to other parts of

Lancashire: James Hargreaves made a machine that makes eight yarns but needs only one spinner.

"Yes," said some people, "but if this goes on, this devilish invention will rob honest handworkers of their living."

If one spinner could do the work which had previously taken eight, then the other seven would soon be out of work — their livelihood would be taken away from them. That is what the weavers and spinners of Lancashire began to fear; and soon somebody else might make a loom on which one man could weave as much as twenty weavers used to do, and then thousands of weavers would be out of work.

This kind of thing could not be allowed to go on; the making of these infernal machines had to be stopped. And so the Lancashire weavers organized a kind of protest march to the village of Blackburn where the Hargreaves lived. A few hundred of them marched and their leaders made fiery speeches: "The machines take the bread from us and from our families, we will be left to starve." The mob roared with anger.

Hargreaves and his wife had wisely left their little cottage and were hiding at a friend's house — otherwise they would have fared ill at the hands of the mob. The furious body of men marched to Hargreaves' cottage, burst open the door and smashed his spinning jenny as well as all the furniture. And while they were at it, they also smashed the looms in Mr Peel's shed. Only when they had broken everything that could be destroyed, did the angry weavers leave Blackburn.

This was the first machine-smashing riot in history, but by no means the last. Later it happened again and again that men put out of work by machines, tried to fight the machines by smashing them — but, of course, it was always in vain. The machines stayed, and the skilled handworkers lost their livelihood.

Hargreaves realized that after this riot, Lancashire was no longer safe for him. He and his wife fled to another part of England, to Nottingham. Now he tried something he should have done before; he tried to take out a patent for his invention — so that anybody who copied the spinning jenny would have to pay him a fee. But you can only get a patent for a machine if no such machine is already in use when you apply for the patent. As spinning jennies were already made and used all over the country, Hargreaves could not get a patent, and so he got nothing for his invention.

And so the Hargreaves remained poor to the end of their lives while others made fortunes. A new class of men was rising in Britain, the manufacturers — men who had the money to have big machines made for them — and they built spinning jennies with twenty spindles.

Another Lancashire inventor, Richard Arkwright, improved the spinning jenny. He had the bright idea to have the spinning wheel not driven by hand or foot, but by water power. For centuries flour mills had used water power to grind corn, now Arkwright used water power to drive the spinning wheel, so even the spinner who used to turn the wheel was no longer necessary. These factories driven by water power were called "mills" — cotton mills or woollen mills — because they worked like flour mills. Power driven machines had arrived.

When Arkwright built such a cotton mill in Lancashire the weavers again protested — they stormed the mill and burnt it down. But Arkwright simply went and built more mills in other parts of England. The new machines had come to stay — and the Industrial Revolution was on its way. Arkwright made a fortune.

It is strange to think that it all began in 1764 in Blackburn where James Hargreaves knocked over his wife's spinning wheel!

37. The Arrival of Steam Power

The stories of Hargreaves and Arkwright show two kinds of inventions which brought about the Industrial Revolution. Hargreaves' invention was a machine which could do the same work as the human hand, but much quicker. His invention increased the speed of production.

Arkwright's use of water power went further: it replaced not only human skill, but human strength and energy with the powers of nature.

It is interesting to follow the stages by which people learned to make the powers of nature work for them. At first they only had their own strength to work with — which is very little compared to the strength of some animals, therefore human beings learned to use certain animals — horses, oxen, donkeys — to work for them. Then came the wind and water — wind to drive sailing ships and mills, water to drive mills. This stage lasted for a long time without much alteration.

Leonardo da Vinci had, however, thought of another way of using water — in the form of steam. He realized that if you heat water, the expanding steam had great power which could be used to move the wheels of machines. He wrote in his notebooks that it would be possible to move a ship over the ocean by steam power. Unfortunately this great idea remained buried in his notebooks.

Two hundred years later, about 1650, a Frenchman, De Cant, was overcome with pity for the poor men who had to row the big ships when there was no wind. He came to the French minister Richelieu with a plan to use steam instead of slaves — and the minister was so upset by the idea of using machines instead of human beings that the poor inventor was thrown into prison for the rest of his life.

Newcomen invented a steam-driven machine which was being used fifty years later, by about 1700, in England. His machine, driven by steam from a water boiler heated by coal, pumped water out of mines. Using a great amount of coal for very little work this wasteful water pump of the English mines was to be the cause of another great step in the Industrial Revolution.

The man who changed the design of this pump and so gave the world a new source of power, was a Scotsman, James Watt. James Watt, who was born in Greenock and lived in Glasgow, had not received a higher education, but being skilled with his hands he had become a maker of scientific instruments for Glasgow University.

At the University there was a model of the steam-driven pump used in the coalmines — and this model had just as many snags and faults as the real pumps used in the mines. One day the Professor of Physics at Glasgow University got so annoyed with the model that he sent for James Watt and said: "Look here, you are the instrument maker. Can you do something with this contraption — change the design, so that it will work smoothly and without hitch?"

The year 1764 when Watts started to fiddle about with that model of the water pump was the same year in which Hargreaves began to fiddle about with his wife's spinning wheel.

But Watt's task was more difficult than Hargreaves'. It took Watt several years (up to 1769) until he hit upon a design which made the machine run more smoothly and efficiently, that is, using far less coal. This design was the first really useful steam engine.

It is not true, as is often said, that Watt "invented" the steam engine — it existed already. What Watt did was to change and improve its design. But Watt realized that his new design was not merely an improved pump, he realized that his design could be used to make steam drive any kind of machine.

And so he went straight to London to take out a patent for his invention. In London he met an engineer, Matthew Boulton, and the two men went into partnership and founded an engineering firm, Boulton and Watt, which became world famous for making steam engines.

The people who first became interested in buying that new steam engine were the mill owners, the cotton manufacturers.

Arkwright's idea of having the spinning wheels driven by water power, by streams and rivers, had certain disadvantages. First, the cotton mill had to be built beside the river or stream; secondly, as the water level of a river changed, it was a very irregular source of power, and in many dry summers the mills had to stop completely.

But with a steam engine driven by coal, a factory could be built anywhere near the coal supply and would run in all weathers.

And so, the cotton industry which was growing rapidly, changed from water power to steam power. The cotton factories were still called "cotton mills," though they were no longer real mills by a river; they were built anywhere and driven by steam and coal.

Up to then coal had only been used for heating homes, but now coal became a source of power, steam power. That was the great change brought about by Watt. And soon steam power would bring another great change.

38. The Locomotive

When James Watt went into partnership with the engineer, Boulton, their firm, Boulton and Watt, became world-famous as makers of steam engines. Steam engines revolutionized the cotton industry as cotton mills changed from water power to steam power. As more and more cotton mills were built, more steam engines were required, and the firm of Boulton and Watt flourished.

Boulton and Watt also improved water pumps for mines, and these water pumps were also sold in great numbers. When an engineering firm sells a big machine like a steam engine, it is not just sent to the customer. They also send one or two engineers who see to it that the machine is properly installed and runs smoothly. That job is usually given to the young engineers employed by the makers.

One such engineer at Boulton and Watt was a Scotsman, William Murdoch. Young Murdoch was full of original ideas. When he came to the firm of Boulton and Watt and applied for a job he was interviewed by Boulton himself. During the conversation Murdoch — being a little nervous — twiddled his hat in his hands, and the hat fell from his fingers. When the hat hit the ground it made a strange solid thump, not at all like an ordinary hat. It turned out that, being short of money, and a thrifty Scotsman, Murdoch had made himself a hat of wood, turning it on a lathe. Old Boulton was so impressed by this that he engaged Murdoch right away.

On one occasion young Murdoch was sent to Cornwall to install several pumps in a tin mine. The job took several weeks and during that time Murdoch lived in a Cornish village. And while he was in that village he experimented with another of his original ideas in his spare time: if the steam engine is not placed on the ground, as it is always done, but mounted on wheels, can it turn the wheels so that the machine moves itself? Murdoch

found a way of doing this by connecting the "piston" of the
steam engine (the part that goes up and down) by iron rods to
the front wheels. He worked it all out on paper first — and then
he made a little model of the whole contraption — just large
enough to see if it would really work with coal and water.

But he did not want to try out his little model in the village,
as the Cornish peasants there were still very ignorant and
Murdoch did not want to scare them. Instead he experimented
at night and in a quiet lane that people seldom frequented. But
one night the little machine ran away from him and clattered
down the lane, spouting smoke and sparks. Just at that moment
the vicar of the village came up the lane. When he saw a dark
object belching smoke and sparks running towards him, he gave
one yelp: "the Devil!" and ran. The village talked for weeks of
nothing else.

Still, the little model worked, and when Murdoch returned
to his firm, Boulton and Watt, he showed it to old Watt and
asked for permission to make further experiments with a steam
engine that would drive itself.

You should have heard Watt! He said it was a disgrace that an
engineer employed by the respectable firm of Boulton and Watt
wasted his time on such nonsense. And that was that. Young
Murdoch had built the first locomotive in Britain — but nothing came of it because old Watt could see no use for it. (In Paris
a Frenchman had made himself a steam driven carriage twenty
years earlier — but it toppled over in the street — and that was
the end of that experiment.)

Murdoch, discouraged by Watt, gave up his idea of a steam
driven carriage, but another man carried on with it. He was a
Cornishman, Richard Trevithick.

Trevithick built the first large size locomotive. It ran on rails
and pulled trucks in an iron mine. Before the locomotive, horse
drawn carts had been used in this mine; and the miners were
furious that the horse drivers had been put out of work. So, in
order to avoid violence, this first railway had to be stopped.

Trevithick made another attempt to use a steam carriage. He
went to London where he built a kind of "merry-go-round" —
a circular track on which a locomotive went round and round —

and people could ride on it for a shilling. But as the speed of that ride was only five miles per hour (8 kph), it was not a great thrill. Trevithick lost money on this venture and eventually gave up. He left England and went to South America.

The man who took up the idea and made a success of it was George Stephenson. He was not — as people often say — the inventor of the locomotive, no more than Watt was the inventor of the steam engine. But, like Watt, Stephenson improved the design so that the locomotive became more than a toy.

The first railway line was built by Stephenson in 1825 between Stockton and Darlington, a stretch of about twenty miles (30 km). You can get some idea of the speed of this locomotive from the fact that a man on horseback rode in front of it to make sure that the line was clear.

It was once again the cotton manufacturers who became interested in this new machine. The only way to move the bales of raw cotton from the port of Liverpool to Manchester, for instance, where most of the cotton mills were, was by barge on the canals which was terribly slow. It took nearly as long as bringing the cotton from America to Liverpool.

Initially it was for the transport of raw cotton that Stephenson built a railway line between Liverpool and Manchester. The line was opened in 1830, and his famous locomotive (there was only one) was called the Rocket. At that time it was the fastest thing on wheels: it could do thirty miles per hour (50 kph).

At first this railway was only used for goods, for cotton, but soon coaches for passengers were added. The first class coaches had cushioned seats and roofs, the second class had wooden seats and no roof, and there was also a third class, no seats and no roof. Imagine what it was like in the roofless coaches on a cold rainy day — and with thick smoke enveloping the passengers!

The success of this Liverpool to Manchester line proved that the steam driven locomotive could move goods as well as passengers both cheaper and faster than anything known before.

Railways now began to spread all over the country, and changed the centuries-old way of life. When people still travelled by horse-drawn coaches from Edinburgh to London the journey took about two weeks and was pretty expensive too. But with the arrival of the railway, the four hundred mile (650 km) journey only took a day. People could move cheaply and quickly from place to place. And people who had never left their town or village before, ventured far afield for little money.

Soon Leonardo da Vinci's dream was to come true too — and steam driven ships would take the place of sailing ships.

At first, George Stephenson's invention found some opposition. For instance, when Bavaria was to build its first railway line, the Government asked the opinion of the Council of Doctors. And the learned medical experts gave it as their opinion that it was unhealthy for the human nervous system to move at such great speeds as thirty miles per hour (50 kph). And if the Government did build such a railway line, it should be boarded up on either side — so that people would not see the landscape rushing past and become giddy.

It is only four or five generations ago that the Industrial Revolution brought the steam engines and locomotives that changed people's way of life completely.

39. The Proletarians

At the time of the Industrial Revolution, there was also a great change in British agriculture, in farming. Most of the land belonged to noblemen, to lords, to the "Squire" as the peasants called him. The squire did not work the land himself — the land was "let" to "tenant farmers" who worked the land, sold what they could and paid a rent to the squire.

Such an "estate" was usually divided into three large fields. Two fields grew crops and the third was grass and weeds. The reason for this was that if you grew wheat year after year, the soil became dead and useless. So the farmers grew their wheat in every field for two years and the third year the field was left fallow, was given a rest. So the three fields were first year crop, second year crop and fallow field.

In the two planted fields each tenant farmer had his own little strip, and the third field was common grazing for their livestock, cows, goats, sheep.

But this changed when the landowners wanted the fallow field to be used for new crops which enriched the soil: turnips and clover. Turnips and clover were new in Britain — they were brought from the Continent — and they replenished the soil with the nitrates that wheat takes from it.

The poorer tenants could not do this; to plough and look after a third field required more work than they could manage. They had no money to pay farmhands and as there was no fallow field, they could not keep animals. Thus it was that thousands of poor tenants had to leave the land, because there was no longer a livelihood for them. So the old way of farming came to an end — only a few rich tenants remained, their fields becoming bigger by taking on the abandoned ones.

Thousands of poor families came to the towns desperate to make a living, and found work there.

The number of cotton mills had grown and grown — the

whole world was buying the new, cheap, factory-made cotton from Britain. Money came pouring into Britain, and the manufacturers built new factories from the money they made.

The more cotton mills that went up, the more workers and machines that were needed. So the machine makers, the engineering firms, prospered and grew and employed more and more people. The iron foundries where iron ore was turned into iron and steel also had to produce more, and employed more and more workers.

Before the Industrial Revolution, let us say in the year 1750, three quarters of Britain's population lived in the country and only one quarter lived in towns, so Britain was an agricultural country at that time. A hundred years later, by 1850, the industrial cities had drawn in the larger part of the population, and Britain had become an industrial nation.

The coming of the machines brought money pouring into Britain and it brought work to thousands, then hundreds of thousands, and then to millions, but now we must consider the conditions in which the factory workers lived, so we can see the other face, the hideous face of the Industrial Revolution.

Before Hargreaves made his spinning jenny, the weavers and spinners lived in their cottages in the country and although they were poor, they lived a simple, healthy life in the clear country air. Each weaver was his own master who could begin or end his work when he liked.

However, after the great change it was different. To get steam for the steam engines that drove the wheels, coal was burnt, and where coal was burnt there was smoke. As the cotton mills grew and spread, the number of tall chimney stacks which poured black smoke into the air until it darkened the sky also grew and spread, and to work in a cotton mill now meant to work in a town of perpetual gloom where the air was thickened by coal and cotton dust.

When a new cotton mill went up, it would need hundreds of workers and these workers would want to live near the mill. So the builders or sometimes the mill owners bought up land as close to the mill site as possible. And on this land they built rows of houses which were planned to crowd as many people as possible, into the smallest space possible.

The builders had a free hand; there were no rules or laws how they should build, so ugly towns were built, and in them the overcrowded tenements soon became slums.

And so, over the green hills of England there spread a cloud of smoke which never lifted. And below the cloud there stood, row upon row of the ugliest buildings ever to disgrace the world.

The rooms in these houses had no ventilation, no water, and no lavatory. For a whole street there was one water pump at one end which was the only water supply for all needs of all the people in the street. And at the other end of the street there was a shed with a hole in the ground — that was the lavatory for the whole street. Each patch of ground between the rows of houses was used as a refuse dump and covered with heaps of rubbish and filth.

Inside the houses, every small room, including the cellars, contained an average of ten people. The people who lived in these conditions, hordes of ragged women, dirty children, were completely cut off from any education or culture.

At that time a new name was given to this class of dirty, working people, they were called "proletarians." The better class of people who did not have to live in the slums were firmly convinced that it was good for the proletarians to work endless hours in the factories — because, if they had more leisure they would only become worse.

In the midst of these slums there stood the gaunt, smoke-blackened factories, and when the workers walked to the factory, the smoke was often so thick that they had to grope their way through the darkness.

Inside the factory the hot air produced by the coal-furnace was thick with floating bits of cotton fibre which got into people's throats and brought on fits of coughing. In this atmosphere men, women and children from the age of five, worked six days a week from 5 am till 8 pm — fifteen hours per day, with only a half hour's break at midday.

All day long the noise of coughing accompanied the clanging

and rattling of the machines. If a child could not get rid of the fibres in its throat by coughing they were given a glass containing a mixture of mustard and water. This horrible mixture made the child sick and expelled the fibres.

There were no seats in the factory — there was no rest — and the foremen went round, armed with a big cane which came down mercilessly on any man, woman or child who faltered in their work.

And what was the reward these "proletarians" received for their work? The average pay was very little.

To keep these factories going, more and more coal had to be brought up from the mines — and the working conditions in the coal mines were even worse than in the factories.

In the coal mines, the digging was done by men, but for other work young children were used. In the underground tunnels children were chained to coal trucks and had to pull them. In many tunnels the ceiling was so low that the children had to crawl for miles on their hands and knees, drawing the heavy coal trucks after them.

They started work before sunrise and came out after dark so that they saw the sun only on Sundays. As they were undernourished, breathed air full of coal dust, and had to do work beyond their strength, these children did not live very long. Thousands died — and those who survived were often crippled.

That was what the Industrial Revolution had brought to Britain. The people who owned the cotton mills, and those who owned the coal mines, grew rich and prosperous. They built themselves beautiful mansions with large parks; they had butlers, footmen, cooks, ladies' maids — a host of servants. And they regarded the inhuman conditions of the proletarians as their lot in life, just as the Romans regarded the condition of slaves.

The production of cotton cloth grew from 27,000 tonnes in 1800 to 70,000 tonnes in 1820, and money came pouring in — but only into the pockets of the factory owners.

40. Liberty and Economics

On the one hand were the cotton manufacturers who amassed fortunes while on the other their workers lived in conditions so inhuman that one can hardly fully imagine them; and the proprietors of coal mines enjoyed every luxury while in their mines, children crawled through tunnels; all the flourishing entrepreneurs enjoyed a prosperity never known before, while hundreds of thousands of fellow human beings — men, women and children — lived as no dog, no criminal, would be allowed to live in modern Britain. If you keep this picture in mind — the life of the property owners, and the life of the proletarians who owned nothing — then you must ask: "Did these prosperous people feel no pity, no compassion? Did they not feel sorry for the unhappy proletarians? Did the prosperous people have no heart for the misery in the slums?"

The answer is that most of them were not cruel monsters, they were not heartless, they did feel pity and sorrow, but they thought that the misery, the poverty and squalor of the proletarians were something that could not be avoided, it was simply their lot, something that could never be changed.

The prosperous people, like the cotton mill owners of Manchester, believed, above all things, in "freedom." A businessman, so they thought — must be free to buy goods at the cheapest price and to sell them at the highest price he can get. The customer, too, is free to buy or not to buy. If the businessman asks too much, the customers will stay away and not buy from him. And so, between them, the businessman and the customer come to a fair price on which they both can agree. This was called: "the free play of the Market." Let the market have a "free play" and all the goods will settle at the right price. So the businessmen believed that in business, in buying and selling, there should be freedom, otherwise there would be no business.

And now we come to the working class, to the proletarians.

The Manchester cotton mill owners said: "The proletarians also have something to sell: their work which means so many hours of their lives — so much energy of their bodies. That's what the proletarian who owns nothing has to sell: a certain portion of his life, a certain portion of his energy. That's what work is. Just as we sell our cotton to customers, so the proletarians sell their work to us. And they are free to sell their work at the best price they can get."

If a cotton manufacturer can't get a high price for his cotton, he must take a low price. If the worker can't get a high wage he must take a low one. That's the free play of the market.

All things which can be bought and sold — cars, houses, apples, clothes — are called "commodities." In ancient Rome slaves too could be bought and sold; slaves then were a "commodity." And the cotton manufacturers, the coal mine proprietors, the machine makers — they all disapproved of slavery, of buying and selling a human being as a "commodity," but they believed quite sincerely that human work (a part of one's lifetime, of one's health and strength) was a commodity. And as other commodities found the right price by the free play of the market — so "work" found its price by the free play of the market.

In business if you buy a commodity you are trying to buy as cheaply as possible, you don't pay a shopkeeper more if you can get the same thing in another shop for much less.

And so it seemed to the business owners quite right that they should buy the commodity "work" as cheaply as possible. After all, if the workers did not like it, they were free to try and get a higher price somewhere else. (Of course, they could not get a better wage anywhere.)

So what was behind the misery of the slums, the suffering of the proletarians, was the quite sincere belief in freedom, in liberty in business, in economics.

We saw that putting liberty, equality, fraternity in the wrong places during the French Revolution created chaos and the massacres of the guillotine.

And now we see that by putting "liberty" into business, into economics, it produced untold misery during the Industrial Revolution. The Industrial Revolution — just like the French

Revolution created misery and suffering because people — at any rate, the business people put "liberty" in the wrong place.

The business people, the cotton manufacturers were not cruel monsters, they honestly believed in freedom — unfortunately in the wrong place. And they believed, therefore, that the terrible life of the proletarians could not be changed; if you changed it, you would interfere with "freedom."

And strangely enough they were confirmed in their belief by a churchman, by a minister of the Church of England, the Rev Thomas Malthus. Malthus wrote a book in which he said that there is never, at any time, enough food for all people in the world, and so there are always some who have to starve. He said, there is never enough cloth, never enough houses — and so some must go in rags, some must live ten or twenty to a room. There is never enough money — and so some must be poor.

This servant of God, went on to say that it had always been so, there was always what he called "a surplus population," extra people for whom there is not enough food or clothes or houses or money. This surplus population was meant to live and die in misery, that was the law of nature, and therefore a law of God. It would be wrong to interfere with this law, it would be wrong to help this "starving surplus population" by charity, by gifts, they were condemned to hunger and misery by a law of nature. It was the duty of those who had a fair share — so said the Rev Malthus — to let the others starve.

Now the wealthy classes of Britain had a clergyman's word for it that it was right, a law of nature, that the working class people should exist in misery.

But not all the rich people fell into this very convenient trap, not all business men made the mistake of placing liberty alongside economics, not all made the mistake of believing that human work was a "commodity" to be bought and sold.

It is a mistake, of course, because a day, an hour of a short human life is so precious that no money can pay for it. Not all rich people made these mistakes though. There was one man, a Welshman, who fought against these mistakes and showed by practical demonstration how wrong they were.

41. Robert Owen

At the time of the Industrial Revolution a new class of people was created — the factory workers, the working class or the "proletarians" as they were called. And, on the other side a new class also appeared — the owners of cotton mills, of other factories, or coal mines and iron mines, the owners of great estates, or the owners of houses which were let. All these people who owned property of one kind or another — and who made money out of this property, were called "capitalists." Capital is any money which is not used for spending, but "invested," buying something that will in time bring more money.

At the time of the Industrial Revolution Britain became divided into capitalists, middle class and working class. But it was possible for a man to make his way from the working class to the capitalists. Such a man was Robert Owen.

Born in 1771 in Wales, Robert Owen's family was so poor that the boy had to earn his own living as a shop assistant from the age of ten. As a shop assistant the little boy had to work from 8 am to 10 pm and the wage he got was only 10 shillings per week, which was very little. But Robert Owen had his mind on getting on in life. He saved a little money, left Wales and travelled to Manchester which was the centre of the cotton industry, and a place where you could see both the misery of the working class and the splendid life of the capitalists. Robert Owen — he was fifteen years old then — saw how money was made. He saw that one pound of raw cotton (it looks like dirty cotton wool) was worth 25 pence, but once this pound of cotton was woven and spun and had become cotton cloth it was worth £5, a difference of £4.75. And the largest part of this enormous profit went into the pockets of the man who owned the machines that did the spinning and weaving.

And so Robert Owen, still working as a shop assistant, saved every penny he could from his wages. He denied himself any pleasure that cost money, and in five years — at the age of twenty — he bought three spinning machines, and engaged a few workers to run them. He had become a "capitalist," a manufacturer in his own right.

Now among the big cotton mills of Manchester, Robert Owen's little factory was very small, and although he made a fair living, he could hardly make a fortune. However, he gained a good reputation for efficiency and for honesty, and it was due to this reputation that the owner of a very large cotton mill offered him the very highly paid job of manager of his mill. Robert Owen sold his little factory and became the highly respected manager of one of the largest mills in Manchester at the age of twenty-two.

For a young man without education or training, Robert Owen had gone far, but there was more good fortune in store for him. At that time cotton mills also spread to Scotland and the largest Scottish cotton mills were in New Lanark on the Clyde.

The owner of these Scottish mills in New Lanark was David Dale who had an only daughter. In the course of some business Robert Owen came from Manchester to New Lanark and met Miss Dale. They fell in love and he married her. He became first a partner (joint owner), and when Mr Dale died, owner of Scotland's largest cotton mills.

So far the story of Robert Owen is just a success story — the story of a young, ambitious man who had good qualities and who was extremely lucky. But there was another side to Robert Owen.

Unlike other cotton manufacturers he felt a deep concern about the miserable, inhuman conditions in which the workers lived. What could be done to help them? Pay them higher wages? That would not really make much difference. No, higher wages alone was not enough, the whole way of life should be changed. And slowly — it was not a sudden idea — slowly Robert Owen formed his plan to set up a new community that should be a model for the working class people everywhere.

Robert Owen started by re-building his workers' houses; in these new houses every family had two rooms — something unheard of among workers in those days. But these people were not used to "cleanliness," what could one do to make them keep the rooms clean? Owen did not want to force his workers to do this or that — he wanted their co-operation. And so the workers elected amongst themselves "inspectors" who visited all the houses regularly. They wrote into a little book which family had a clean home, and which had a dirty one. That was quite enough — for no woman could bear to be put down as a dirty housewife while her neighbour got good marks for cleanliness.

In the factory too Robert Owen had his own way of encouraging good work. There were boards of different colours in every factory, black, blue, red, yellow, white. People who worked very badly had their names written on the black board, and the best workers on the white one. Of course, the lazy workers were soon ashamed of being on black or blue boards week after week, and changed. Thus the standard of work in Owen's factories became higher than anywhere else in the cotton industry.

In other places the shops where the workers bought food or clothes were run by unscrupulous shopkeepers who overcharged and cheated, but not in New Lanark. Robert Owen put up shops which bought all goods cheaply at wholesale prices and sold them without profit to the workers. These stores of Robert Owen were the beginning of the Co-operative (Co-op) Stores which, later, spread all over Britain. The Co-op movement started with Robert Owen's shops in New Lanark.

No one had given any thought to how a worker could live if he fell ill. But Robert Owen thought of it. Partly from the workers' money and partly from his own, he started a "sickness fund" as it was called — money that was put aside for sick workers and their families.

But Robert Owen's special concern was the children. No child under the age of ten was allowed to work in his factories (remember that he himself had started at ten and so he did not think it wrong). But the children from ten to fifteen who did work in the factory only worked for five hours.

No one had given a thought to the education of working class children, but Robert Owen did. He built a school in New Lanark that was more than a hundred years ahead of its time.

His idea was that a school should not only teach this or that subject, but that it should also form the children's character. To beat a child, to use a cane or strap, is not the way to build up a strong character — it produces cowards or bullies. And so in this school in New Lanark there was no corporal punishment, which was quite unusual in those days.

Robert Owen also believed that music and even dancing was essential in a child's education, and so music and folk-dancing were part of the weekly lessons.

New Lanark gradually became a model community of healthier and happier people due to the change in social conditions implemented by Robert Owen. Undoubtedly his workers were grateful for what he had done for them and their children.

Robert Owen had given the right answer to the wrong theories, the answer that the world of industry, or economics needs co-operation, one could say he was a hero of brotherhood, of fraternity. He, the capitalist had worked in co-operation, in the spirit of brotherhood, with his workers.

Robert Owen had hoped his model community in New Lanark would be copied by others in Britain, but he was mistaken. No other factory owner copied him. In his disappointment Robert Owen made a great mistake — he tried to set up a much larger community in America. This new experiment in the New World, called "New Harmony" was, unfortunately, a failure. He lost all his money, had to sell New Lanark and died in poverty in 1858.

And under the new owners, New Lanark went back to the bad old ways. Yet, Robert Owen had not lived and worked in vain, he had shown that the Industrial Revolution demanded co-operation, brotherhood, in industry, in economics.

42. The Workers' Struggle

Robert Owen was in his own way, a genius. Long before that time another genius, Leonardo, had many ideas which were far ahead of his time: in Leonardo's own time his ideas could not yet be put into practice, and it was the same with Robert Owen. In his own time people thought he was a crank and took little notice of what he did at New Lanark. However, many of Owen's ideas were eventually put into practice.

His non-profit stores were the beginning of the Co-op Stores which spread all over Britain. And the "sick fund" for his workers was the beginning of the National Health Service.

There was another idea of Robert Owen's which was not realized in his own time.

To understand this idea, remember an incident from the early days of the locomotive. Richard Trevithick had built a railway for an iron mine. But the workers protested against it, because it put the driver of horse drawn carts out of work. And, since all the workers stood together in this matter, the owner had to give in and the railway was removed.

On his own a worker was quite powerless, he was at the mercy of the capitalist, the factory owner. But whenever the workers of a factory or a mine acted together they had power, they could force the owner to take notice of their wishes.

The incident with the railway in the iron mine was one of many which took place in cotton mills, steel works, coal mines. From all these incidents the workers learnt the lesson: that only by standing together, by acting in union could they hope to improve the terrible conditions in which they lived.

And so the workers of one mine, of one cotton mill, or of one steel works, joined together and formed what they called "unions." But these little unions of a single cotton mill or a single coal mine had neither much power nor much money. Regarding small matters they could persuade or force a manufacturer to take notice of the workers' wishes, but when it came to important matters, like higher wages or better living-conditions, the little unions could do nothing. If his workers made a nuisance of themselves, the owner could always sack them, send them away and get new workers from the crowded slums. So the small unions of each single factory or mine could do nothing towards a real improvement in the conditions of the workers.

And now we come back to Robert Owen who was so concerned with the terrible conditions of the workers. It was his idea that all the small unions of the cotton mills should co-operate and form one large union, the Trade Union for *all* the cotton workers. And all the small unions of the coal mines should co-operate and work together in one great trade union of all coal miners — and so on.

Such a trade union was much more powerful than the smaller ones that had gone before. If a mill owner sacked all his workers he could not get any other, for the trade union forbade its members to work for that owner.

The trade unions which became very powerful organizations were the idea of Robert Owen who was really a capitalist himself, but one who realized that co-operation and brotherhood, is the right principle in economics.

The workers took to this idea, and every small union of a single factory became a branch of the great national trade union. But at this stage the Government stepped in and made a law forbidding trade unions.

In those days not every person in Britain could vote at election times, only the people who owned property: a house, a shop, a farm, a factory. If you didn't even own the house you lived in — like the workers — you had no voting right. And whatever government was elected, was on the side of the property-owners, not on the side of the workers who could not even vote.

The trade unions would have given power to the working class, and the Government would not stand for this. And so all unions were forbidden by law and, for the time being, Robert Owen's idea came to nothing.

In 1815 when Napoleon was finally defeated at Waterloo, Britain could look forward to a period of peace. But to the cotton workers, peace brought only worse misery than before. During the war with Napoleon the British Army and Navy had needed hundreds of thousands of uniforms, and the cotton industry had flourished — the mills employed as many people as they could get and they had even paid them a little more than usual. But as soon as the war was over, there was no longer any need for uniforms. The demand reduced their production, and hundreds of thousands of cotton workers were sacked — they were no longer wanted. There was no pay for anybody out of work, and if the unemployed cotton workers starved to death then, as the Rev Malthus had said, it was simply a law of nature; sad, but it could not be helped.

But even the workers still employed in the cotton mills suffered for now they were paid much less than before. If a man said that he could not live on the reduced wage, the answer was that there were thousands willing to work for even less. But while the wages dropped the food prices went up. And so the misery, the hunger, the suffering of the cotton workers was worse than it had ever been before.

It is no wonder that some stood up and preached to the crowds of ragged and starving men and women, that only an armed rising, a revolution like the French Revolution, could help him.

And so on August 16, 1819, the cotton workers of Manchester held a great protest meeting at St Peter's Field, just outside Manchester. About eighty thousand people, men and women came: they had no weapons, but they marched to the meeting in columns of five, like soldiers, to the tune of drums and bugles, and they carried the red, white and blue banners of the French Revolution.

The vast numbers of the demonstrators, and their menacing looks terrified the well-to-do shopkeepers and all the wealthy citizens of Manchester who demanded protection. And so a cavalry regiment was sent to keep law and order.

When the red-coated soldiers arrived at St Peter's Field, the crowd of cotton workers remained quite orderly, except for shouting some abuse. But then one cotton worker mounted a platform to make a speech.

At that moment the officer in charge of the soldiers gave the order: Arrest this man! And the line of red coats drew their swords and rode into the crowd. A great roar of anger rose from the people, they tried to stop the horsemen by clutching at bridles and stirrups, and the soldiers hit out with their swords. They rode down people who barred the way. And then the crowd panicked. People tried to run away and in the rush hundreds were trampled down. When the field was cleared, it was littered with the bodies of dead and injured people.

This was the Massacre of Peterloo, as it was called by the workers who compared it with bitter humour with Waterloo.

But this terrible, shameful event did one thing: it roused the conscience of the British people. Even the wealthy landowners and business people realized now that the living conditions of the workers had to be changed. And gradually laws came which did away with the worst evils of the Industrial Revolution. In 1824 Trade Unions were made legal, and in 1833 child labour was reduced to ten hours a day.

Around that time when the English Parliament was very slowly and hesitatingly improving things for the workers, in 1845 Karl Marx, a German, arrived in England. Even then, living conditions in the workers' slums were still terrible. And it was with these conditions before him that Karl Marx wrote *Das Kapital,* a book that was to make history. Marx preached that only a ruthless struggle between the classes — between the proletarians and the capitalists — could in the end, after the victory of the workers, produce a new society, a society in which all the good things would be shared fairly by all. This new society in which all property, houses, factories, farms would be "common property" and not owned by capitalists, he called "Communist Society."

With this book which taught the class struggle and the future Communist society, Karl Marx became the founder of Communism.

If Britain had followed the example of Robert Owen, there would have been no Massacre of Peterloo, no class war, but co-operation. But the property-owning classes of Britain believed too long in liberty in the wrong place; they believed too long in the ideas of the Rev Malthus — that the surplus population was doomed to suffer — and so instead of Robert Owen's ideas, it was Karl Marx's that spread in the world. And this led to the Communist states like Russia, China and the terrible division of the world in the second half of the twentieth century. It all started with the Industrial Revolution.

43. Robert Clive

Cotton played a decisive part in the Industrial Revolution: It was the spinning of cotton that was first mechanized by Hargreaves, it was for cotton spinning that Arkwright built the first mills by a river, it was the cotton mills which first bought Watt's steam engine, and it was the cotton manufacturers who first saw the advantages of Stephenson's railway. Every step on this road of the Industrial Revolution was in one way or another connected to cotton.

But it was also the cotton workers who had the first and worst slums, and it was the misery of the cotton workers that inspired Robert Owen, a cotton manufacturer, to try his experiment at New Lanark. It was also the misery of the cotton workers that gave Robert Owen the idea of trade unions, and it was this misery that led to the Massacre of Peterloo in the centre of the cotton trade.

Of course, the Industrial Revolution not only took place in the cotton industry, it soon gripped every kind of production. But cotton was the power that set the Industrial Revolution moving, it was the first mechanized industry. And it was the export of cotton that initially brought money pouring into England.

Just think — cotton does not grow in Britain, all that Britain had (before other countries caught up) were the machines, the industry for weaving and spinning, yet these industries brought great wealth to Britain.

It was cotton that began and developed the Industrial Revolution. By a strange coincidence — or perhaps it was not quite such a coincidence — it was just at the time when the Industrial Revolution gathered momentum that Britain took possession of a large cotton producing land, in fact the homeland of cotton, the land which had grown and used cotton before any other, a land that was considered a most valuable treasure, the land of India.

The conquest of India by the British was mainly due to the courage and enterprise of one man, Robert Clive.

Robert Clive was born before the Industrial Revolution began, in 1725. His parents were well-to-do people and their only worry was their son, Robert, who did everything to drive them and his teachers to despair. At school he showed no interest, no will to learn anything. The only thing he did enjoy was fighting with other boys, nothing else. By the time he was eighteen his parents were only too glad to find a job for him that took him far away from them, a job in India.

India was at that time not one country but was divided into many independent states. Between these separate states, ruled by Maharajahs, there was perpetual rivalry and war. And the European nations, specially Britain, Portugal, Holland and France only had small colonies on the coast. But by helping one Maharajah against another — and getting more land as reward — the European powers tried to make their colonies larger.

Clive was sent as a clerk, an office worker, to the British colony of Madras in India, He had to write out long lists of stores, and he was not made for this tedious kind of job. He became so desperate he would have run away — but where to? He had no money, no skill, no education. In his despair he decided to commit suicide. One day he was alone in his office, he loaded his pistol, put it against his head and pulled the trigger. There was a click, but no explosion. Perhaps he had not loaded it properly. He took the bullets out, reloaded and tried a second time. But again it produced only a click and no bullet. Disgusted, Clive put the pistol down. At this moment a friend came into the office. Clive said: "Look at this pistol, it doesn't work and I don't know why." The friend took the pistol, pointed it out of the window and pulled the trigger, and "bang" went the bullet out through the window.

The next day Clive was offered a chance to leave the tedious office job. Fighting had broken out between two Indian States. One state was helped by the British, the other by the French. And if Clive wished, he could become a soldier and help Britain's ally. At long last Clive could do what he loved doing: fighting.

He was put in charge of five hundred men — two hundred British and three hundred Indians. His first task was to take a fortress, called Arcot, which he stormed with very little loss of life. But he had hardly taken possession of the fortress when he received the news that an army of ten thousand was approaching. Five hundred against ten thousand! Another man would have speedily withdrawn, but not Clive.

He gathered food, strengthened the fortifications — and got ready for a long siege. And it was a long siege. For seven weeks the enemies held the fortress surrounded, hoping to starve the defenders into surrender. But, though food was running short, Clive and his men held out. After these seven weeks the enemies lost patience and made an all-out attack. But Clive had prepared for it — and his cannons created such havoc amongst the attackers that, having lost half their men, they gave up the siege and marched away in 1751. It was a great victory for Clive and made his name famous throughout India.

He won a few more victories and the Indians soon came to believe that Clive was invincible. Under his leadership, the British began to conquer one Indian state after another. The conquest of India had begun.

However, for health reasons, Clive had to interrupt his campaigns. He went home on leave to England where he was given a hero's welcome. In his absence the Indian Ruler of Bengal attacked one of the oldest British colonies, the port of Calcutta. The city was completely taken by surprise — there was only time to put the British women and children on the only boat that was available to send them back to England. The captain refused to wait for the men, and sailed away. Calcutta then surrendered. There were about a hundred and fifty British in Calcutta and on the order of the Indian Prince, Nawab Siraj-ad-Dawla, they were all driven into a windowless prison cell, 18 by 15 feet (6 x 5 m). They were pushed in, crammed together like sardines in a tin, and the door was locked. It was summer and even out in the open, the heat was unbearable; in the prison it was worse than hell. Gasping for breath, raging with thirst, the prisoners cried out for air, for water, in vain.

Next morning the Indian guards opened the door again —

only twenty out of the hundred and fifty prisoners were still alive. That was the famous — or infamous Black Hole of Calcutta.

At the news of the treacherous attack, Clive returned to India. It was only a few hundred British and loyal Indian troops he led against the great army of the Bengal ruler, an army which included elephants, camels, horses, cannons. In the Battle of Plassey, Clive won a resounding victory, losing only twenty men while the enemy lost hundreds. The Indian prince fled, but one of his own ministers, in order to gain the favour of the British, killed him and so made him pay for the Black Hole of Calcutta.

Once the great and powerful state of Bengal was in British hands, no other state of India could hope to hold out, and gradually the entire subcontinent became a British colony (only becoming independent in 1947). And all this began with Robert Clive.

Yet, the end of this great man's life was tragic. When Clive returned again to England he left men in charge of India who were dishonest, who accepted bribes and used their positions to get rich. Clive was accused in the British Parliament of having taken a share in these "rackets." He proved his innocence and in the end, Parliament thanked him for his great services. But he was so depressed by the fact that the newspapers and MPs had accused him of dishonesty that once again, he decided to take his own life. This time, however, the pistol did fire when he pulled the trigger.

As the Industrial Revolution made Britain one of the wealthiest countries in the world, so the conquest of India made her one of the most powerful nations in the world. The nineteenth century was the time when Britain rose to the rank of a world power whose ships sailed on every sea, and whose soldiers guarded vast colonies in every continent.

44. Garibaldi: the Early Years

We have looked at the events which made Britain a world power in the nineteenth century, the Industrial Revolution and the conquest of India. At the same time this great and wealthy nation had a working class that lived in misery because the ruling classes had no understanding of the idea of brotherhood, of co-operation in economics.

Now we come to heroes of freedom, of liberty. For this we look at other countries at the time when Britain was going through the Industrial Revolution.

In other parts of Europe, such as Italy, there came another kind of revolution, a revolution more concerned with liberty than with fraternity. At that time Italy was not just one country, but was divided into separate states, each with its own ruler. In the South there was the Kingdom of Naples ruled by a Spanish Prince. There was the whole North of Italy which was not independent at all but was ruled by Austria. One part, called Piedmont had an Italian King, and another part was ruled by the Pope in Rome. Italy was broken up like a jigsaw puzzle.

But, after the Napoleonic Wars, specially amongst the young, there grew a great desire, a great longing, to be one nation, under one government. You can imagine that this was not to the liking of the rulers of each state. The Emperor of Austria did not want to lose his part of Northern Italy, the King of Piedmont did not want to give up his throne, and so the young men who spoke openly of a united Italy were arrested and thrown into prison.

Some of the young hot-heads still continued to meet secretly. But as they wrote each other letters about their hopes for a united Italy, the oppression became worse. No one was allowed to give a party or hold a meeting without permission by the police. Every letter sent by post was opened by police officers and if it contained dangerous ideas the writer of the letter was arrested and sent to prison for years. No newspaper and no book could be published that contained any "dangerous" thoughts, or that complained about the oppression. Italy became a land without freedom.

Some young Italians fled to other countries, to France, to Britain, and there they plotted and planned for a free and united Italy. They wrote books which were then smuggled into Italy and passed from hand to hand. All this helped the cause of freedom, it kept the hope for better times alive in the hearts of the people, but it was not enough. What was needed was a man who could lead into battle, a fighter for freedom. Such a man was Guiseppe Garibaldi (1807–82).

Garibaldi's father was a sailor, a simple man who had only one ambition: that his only son should have a good education and become something better than a sailor. But young Garibaldi was not interested in books — he wanted to go to sea. His father would not hear of it. So, at the age of fifteen, Garibaldi persuaded some other boys to run away with him. They stole a small sailing boat and sailed away. However, at the father's request, a coastguard vessel sailed after them and brought the youngsters back.

This little event shows two things about Garibaldi: he was head-strong and he was a leader. In any case, the father realized that such a boy would never make a good lawyer or doctor, and let him go to sea.

It was on his sailing voyages that at Marseilles, in France, Garibaldi met Italians who had fled from their homeland to work for the revolution, and he became an enthusiastic member of this group of rebels.

As a sailor, Garibaldi had great opportunities to work for the revolution. When his ship came to an Italian port he talked to sailors and fishermen and tried to win them over to the idea of rising against their rulers to free and unite Italy. On one occasion the police discovered what was going on, and although Garibaldi escaped, he was proclaimed a traitor, condemned to death and a reward was offered for his capture. As Italy was no longer safe for Garibaldi, he embarked on a ship sailing to Brazil, to Rio de Janeiro. At this time Brazil was in the throes of a revolution, the people of one province had risen against the Government. Garibaldi immediately joined the rebels — and for the next six years fought against the Government on land and sea.

On one occasion he was taken prisoner, but after a few weeks some people who were secretly on his side helped him to escape. However, he was unlucky; he was caught again before he had gone far. The officer in charge of the prisoners was furious: "Who are the men who helped you to escape?" he shouted. Garibaldi refused to betray his friends. He was beaten with sticks and canes, but still gave no answer. Then the officer tried a worse torture. At his order Garibaldi was hung up by his hands from a beam. The excruciating pain in his arms made Garibaldi faint, but he did not give away his friends. He was taken down and thrown into his cell. Two weeks later he escaped again — and this time he got away.

He continued fighting on the side of the rebels and was given command of a ship. One day he was on deck of this ship, watching the coast through a telescope. He saw a big house and on the balcony there stood a girl. He could see her quite clearly through his telescope, and as soon as he saw her he said to himself: "This is the girl I am going to marry."

At his order the ship stopped. A boat was lowered and Garibaldi rowed ashore. He searched everywhere for the house he had seen through the telescope, but could not find it. He was just about to give up when he met with another rebel officer he knew who said: "I am just about to visit friends who have a house nearby, come with me, they will be pleased to meet you."

Garibaldi accepted the invitation and accompanied the officer — and when they came to the house, the first person he saw was the girl he had watched through the telescope. For a full minute Garibaldi and the girl looked at each other without saying a word. As they both said later, they felt as if they were not meeting for the first time but had known each other a long, long time ago. At last Garibaldi found his voice and his first words to this girl — on whom he had set eyes only that morning — were: "You must become my wife."

The girl answered only with a nod and a smile. Thus began their great romance.

The girl's name was Anita Ribera; she was only eighteen and her father had promised her to a man she did not love. The man she now saw before her, Garibaldi was already famous for his daring; he had a head like a lion, with flowing fair hair, a beard the colour of gold, and eyes of deep blue. He was tall and strong and looked every inch what he was: a reckless adventurer. Anita knew, from the moment of this first encounter, that she would marry this man and no other, but that her father would never consent to her marrying a foreign adventurer.

Shortly after this strange first meeting, Anita eloped with Garibaldi and married him. From then onwards they shared all the dangers and hardships of a life that had more than its fair share of both.

In one battle, the rebels for whom Garibaldi fought were defeated and in the chaos of fleeing troops, Anita was separated from her husband and taken prisoner. But she escaped managed to lasso a horse and rode sixty miles (100 km) through wild country, alone and without food. Twice she had to swim wide rivers by holding on to the horse's mane, but after four days she reached safety and rejoined her jubilant husband.

In another battle Garibaldi was badly wounded and left for dead on the battlefield. When the news of his death was brought to Anita she would not believe it. She said: "My heart would tell me if he were dead, but my heart knows he is still alive."

It was already night when they brought her the news, but she went out into the darkness with a little oil lamp. She went to the battlefield that was covered with hundreds of bodies. And there, alone in the night, she went from corpse to corpse, shining her lamp at the still faces; for hours she stumbled amongst the dead until she found her husband. He was covered with blood, unconscious, but his heart was still beating. She dressed his wounds, then she went to fetch help and for weeks she nursed him back to life.

In the midst of these constant dangers their first child was born. The baby, a boy, was only twelve days old when the rebels suffered a great defeat and Garibaldi and his family had to flee into the Brazilian jungle. It was the rainy season, for weeks they lived in the heavy downpour, soaked to the skin, without proper food, plagued by insects, in constant danger from jungle beasts and snakes as well as enemy troops, and always in fear that the baby might die. But they and the baby survived and escaped.

Garibaldi's time in South America prepared him for the real task that was still ahead, the task of leading a revolution in Italy against the tyrants who kept the country divided and the people oppressed.

45. Garibaldi and the Unification of Italy

Before continuing with Garibaldi's biography we must look at conditions in Europe in the first half of the nineteenth century. After the French Revolution all the rulers in Europe, kings, emperors, tsars, feared that these dangerous ideas of liberty, equality and fraternity, would spread to their own lands and that they, too, would lose their thrones and even their lives. And so they all took measures to keep their subjects quiet by instilling fear in them. The oppression in Italy was similar in France, in Germany, in Austria, in Russia. Speaking or writing about freedom was enough to send a man to prison. The police were not there to protect the people but to arrest and imprison and execute anybody who was suspected of harbouring dangerous ideas. Britain was the only country where people could speak their mind. Elsewhere in Europe there was neither free speech, nor freedom to write or print anything that was not to the liking of the monarchs.

But oppression, police and persecution cannot stop ideas. It has never worked in the long run; only for a while. In Europe it worked for quite a while, until 1848. The year 1848 is one of the years in history which should be written in red — it was a year of revolutions.

It all started in France. In February 1848 the French revolted against King Louis Philippe (a relative of Louis XVI) and he fled to England. And the success of this uprising sparked revolutions all over Europe; in Vienna the students led a revolution against Ferdinand, Emperor of Austria, but they were unlucky, after heroic fighting they were overpowered by troops and many students were executed. In Germany, too, a revolution broke out, but was quelled by the armed forces.

And now we come to Italy. The North of Italy was a part of

the Austrian Empire, but against the wishes of the Italian people. And in this year of revolutions, 1848, the people of Northern Italy rose in rebellion against the Austrians.

What about the rest of Italy? There was one kingdom, the Kingdom of Piedmont, where the King, Charles Albert, rather unexpectedly declared himself for the rebels and willing to fight on their side for a free and united Italy, and promised to give it a parliament as Britain had.

Thus we can return to Garibaldi. With a revolution in Italy raging, and a king siding with the rebels, nothing could have kept him and faithful Anita in America. Leaving the children with relatives in France, they arrived in Italy full of hope to see the country liberated and united in one nation.

But Garibaldi's hopes and the hopes of the Italian people were bitterly disappointed. The Emperor of Austria, having successfully quashed the students' revolution in Vienna, now raised a large army which came pouring down over the Alps into Northern Italy and crushed the ill-trained and ill-armed Italian rebels. And the King of Piedmont quickly gave in made peace.

And Garibaldi? He and Anita with a small group of faithful followers were left in the lurch. The countryside, the cities in Austrian hands, and the Austrian soldiers were out in force, hunting for that dangerous rebel Garibaldi. There was only one hope for the little group of rebels — to march as fast as they could to the coast and escape on a ship.

And march they did — mile after mile, without rest, onwards before the Austrians could catch up with them. But the hardship of these marches broke Anita's health; she marched bravely on but became weaker and weaker.

At long last they reached the coast and found fishermen willing to help them. At night the little band embarked in half a dozen boats and left the shore. But — to their misfortune — it was a bright moonlit night and as they passed a little promontory, Austrian guns stationed there opened fire. Only one boat carrying Garibaldi, Anita and six men, escaped. All other boats were sunk. The single boat returned to the shore and the survivors scattered in all directions, only one man remained with Garibaldi and Anita. By this time Anita could no longer walk and the two men carried her until they reached a farmhouse. Fortunately, the farmer was an Italian patriot and admirer of Garibaldi. He kept them hidden from the Austrians. They had caught the other survivors and shot them but they still hunted for Garibaldi. They never found him. Anita had gone through too much hardship and, in spite of every care she died on this farm. It was the only time that Garibaldi broke down and wept.

But he could not spare much time for sorrow — he could not even stay to see Anita buried — for the Austrians were still seeking for him and the hide-out was no longer safe. He and his friend had more than one hair-breadth escape but in the end he did get away and left Italy again for many years. Once again he roamed the seas as Captain of trading vessels and came as far as China.

But six years later, in 1854, there came another chance to return to his homeland. An important change had taken place in the Kingdom of Piedmont. A young and courageous king had come to the throne, Victor Emmanuel, who was truly willing to fight for a free and united Italy. But Piedmont could not hope to win against the might of Austria without a powerful ally — and there was such an ally: France.

When Louis Philippe was driven away in the French Revolution of 1848, the French made Louis Napoleon, a nephew of Napoleon Bonaparte, president of the republic. This nephew was, however, just as ambitious as his uncle had been, and after a short time as president, declared himself Emperor of France under the title Napoleon III. (Napoleon's son who had died young was considered Napoleon II). And this new Napoleon was willing to come to the aid of Piedmont in its fight against Austria.

What was still needed was a man to lead the Italians, a man experienced in battle, a man whom they could follow with heart and soul, and that man was Garibaldi. He was called to Piedmont where he started to train a volunteer force of one thousand men specially chosen for fitness and courage. They were given red shirts as a sign of their willingness to give their blood for freedom.

The time of Garibaldi's Redshirts came when a revolution broke out on the island of Sicily. This island was under Spanish rule who were cruel masters. They were certainly inhumanly cruel in their treatment of the people of Sicily. In the end the poor, down-trodden islanders could not stand it any longer and revolted. But the Sicilian peasants would not have had any hope of success if Garibaldi had not come with his Redshirts, and in three months the Spaniards were driven out.

The Kingdom of Naples in the south was also under Spanish rule. Garibaldi and his Redshirts crossed over from Sicily to attack this Kingdom of Naples — but they did not have to do any attacking. The army sent against him surrendered without firing a single shot. The people of Naples rose in rebellion against the Spanish ruler who fled in haste and Garibaldi was welcomed as their liberator.

At this point Garibaldi's fame and popularity was so great that, had he so wished, he could have made himself King of Italy. But this was not in his nature — and he remained faithful to Victor Emmanuel, the King of Piedmont.

In the meantime there was also war in Northern Italy, though Garibaldi took no part in it. In Northern Italy Napoleon III, as he had promised, had come to help the Italians against Austria. In a terrible battle the combined French and Italian troops defeated the Austrians. This Battle of Solferino in 1859 is important for quite another reason which we shall come to.

In any case, after the Battle of Solferino, the north of Italy was also set free, and at long last the great dream of so many Italians came true. In 1861 the whole of Italy was declared one nation — no longer divided into bits and pieces, and the first king of Italy, Victor Emmanuel, gave this new country a parliament, free elections, free speech (as Britain also had). Freedom had come to Italy, and few men had done so much and suffered so much for it as Garibaldi, the hero of freedom.

It is true that in later years Garibaldi quarrelled with King Victor Emmanuel and with the King's ministers, but, then the old rebel was not an easy man to get on with and as stubborn in old age as he was in his youth. But that had also made him a hero of liberty, as Robert Owen was a hero of fraternity.

46. Henri Dunant

We have looked at liberty, equality and fraternity, but these qualities would be incomplete without something else. Like a great river which at its delta divides into three, so liberty, equality, fraternity come from one source, and they cannot exist without that source. The source is charity, or compassion, a deep strong feeling for other people, the ability to share the joys and sorrows of others as if they were one's own. Owen had compassion for his workers, Garibaldi had compassion for his oppressed fellow countrymen in Italy, and it was this which made them heroes of brotherhood or of liberty. Now we shall come to a hero of compassion.

This man was born in Switzerland, in Geneva — a beautiful city on Switzerland's largest lake, the Lake of Geneva. In that part of Switzerland, French is the national language and our hero has a French name Henri Dunant (1828–1910), but he was Swiss.

Dunant was the son of rich business people in Geneva, and as he grew up he showed the makings of a good businessman himself — a man who used money to make more money. But, already as a child, Dunant showed another side. One day, passing by the lake, he saw some boys angling for fish. When they caught one they did not kill it but threw it into a basket where some fish were feebly flapping. Young Dunant could not stand the sight; he went to the boys, gave them whatever pocket money he had on him for the fish and threw the fish back into the lake.

But he had a good brain for business and as a grown up man he became a very wealthy and respected businessman in Geneva. A businessman is always looking for an opportunity to invest money, to multiply it, and so was Dunant. The question was: where would his money bring the largest profit?

Now at that time, rich people, capitalists, like Dunant began to invest money not only in their own countries, not even in Europe, but overseas in colonies. Dunant's own country, Switzerland, had no colonies, but her great neighbour, France, had. It was only natural that Dunant whose mother language was French, should think of a French colony for investing his money. And the nearest French colony was Algeria, on the coast of North Africa.

And so our businessman, Dunant, travelled to Algeria to see for himself whether there were opportunities for investment that would in time bring a good profit. In the end he bought land, large estates with good soil on which wheat could be grown. But he also wanted to build mills where the wheat could be ground, and he wanted to dig canals to have water to drive the mills. To build a canal in Algeria the permission of the French Government in Paris was required. So Dunant wrote to Paris and asked for permission. But no answer came.

Dunant was angry: he had paid most of his fortune for the land and now he was held up by some beaurocrat in an office in Paris. And he decided he would go straight to the head of the French Government, which at that time was the new Emperor, Napoleon III. He would get permission for his canals from the Emperor. So he travelled to Paris, but the Emperor was not there. Napoleon III had marched with his army to Italy to help the Italians against Austria.

But this did not stop Dunant. If Napoleon III was in Italy, he would also go to Italy and get hold of His Majesty there. Dunant travelled to Italy, and in the end, he got as far as the headquarters of the French army just on the evening before the great Battle of Solferino. Of course, no one, least of all the Emperor, had time to listen to Dunant and his complaints; the French were busy getting ready for the coming battle. Dunant had to wait.

And so it came that the next day, June 24, 1859, Dunant had the opportunity to watch the whole battle of Solferino from a hill.

It was June, a hot Italian June, and throughout the day the two armies — the French and Italians on one side, the Austrians on the other — fought a savage, murderous battle in the burning sun.

Lines of men in marching order stormed against each other with the force of a raging torrent. This was a battle with hand-to-hand fighting, men stabbed their enemies with bayonets, they smashed their skulls with rifle-butts, they hacked them down with sabres. And when a man had no weapon left he would seize an enemy by the throat or tear at him with his teeth. It was a battle in which men fought like beasts, without mercy, and even the wounded fought on as long as they had strength. Cavalry horses trampled upon the bodies on the ground, cannon wheels rolled over them. The earth was soaked with blood, and the cries of anguish and pain were at times as loud as the thunder of gunfire.

Towards evening the Austrians were defeated and in full retreat. The battle was over, but not the suffering. Forty thousand wounded, French, Italian, Austrian, were left lying on the battlefield without nurses, doctors, without food or water. Their thirst was far worse than the pain of their wounds, and the whole night the cries of the tormented rent the air. It was so bad that next morning some men were found who had crammed earth into their mouth and who had died in convulsions.

The next day the suffering, the agonies of the wounded continued, for there was still no help for them. They were covered with flies and their wounds festered. On that day the businessman Dunant forgot his business. If no one else did something for the thousands in agony, he would.

He gathered the peasants of a nearby Italian village and organized a band of people to begin the nearly hopeless task. He got the village children to act as water carriers. He sent carts to the nearest town and with his own money bought bandages, pins, sponges, fruit. He got hold of two English tourists and made them join the little band of peasant men and women who attended the wounded. At first the Italian peasants would only look after Italian and French soldiers — they would not help the Austrian enemies. But Dunant cried out *"Tutti fratelli"* (We are all brothers), and the Italian peasants repeated: "It is true, all men are brothers." And they treated the wounded Austrians like their own soldiers. There were forty thousand wounded and only a pitiful little band of volunteers — perhaps a hundred — to help.

For three days these true Christians, driven by the example of Dunant, worked day and night, with no more than an hour's rest now and then. And Dunant managed, at last, to get from the French army horse-carts to take the wounded to the nearest town where schools, churches, town halls, were cleared for them.

But he never saw the Emperor Napoleon III. The Emperor had not liked the sight and had, immediately after the battle, set out for Paris.

But Dunant was no longer interested in his business, in his canals and mills. He returned to Geneva, to Switzerland with only one thought in his mind: "What can I do to help the wounded in future wars, in future battles?" Back in Geneva, he wrote a book, *The Battle of Solferino,* in which he not only described all that had happened, but proposed that all nations should come to an agreement about the treatment of wounded and prisoners.

The book made a deep impression all over the world, but Dunant wanted more than sympathetic feelings, he wanted something to be done. He travelled from one Government to the other, talked with ministers, prime ministers, kings. Finally, in 1864 there was a meeting in Geneva and representatives of many nations signed the Geneva Convention, and the Red Cross was set up. For the first time in history nations had come to agree fully on something — and it was all the work of Dunant. Since then the Red Cross has saved millions of lives.

But while Dunant did all this, he had no time to look after his business, and the result was that he lost all his money and was even left with large debts, he owed people money and could not pay. This was something so shameful for him, that he resigned from the Red Cross — he left the Red Cross so that people should not connect this new organization for the benefit of mankind with a person who could not pay his debts. So, without money, without a job, Dunant became so poor that at one time he had to sleep in the streets. Then he disappeared, people forgot him, and for many years, no one knew whether he still lived or not.

But in 1908 when Dunant was eighty years old, a journalist

discovered him; he was in a village in the Alps. Now gifts, telegrams, from all over the world arrived and Dunant could at least die with the knowledge that he was not forgotten.*

He will never be forgotten — he is one of the great heroes of compassion, of mercy, of love between human beings.

* Dunant was awarded the first Nobel Prize for peace in 1901.

47. Abraham Lincoln

Robert Owen was a hero of fraternity, and Garibaldi a hero of liberty. Now we come to our hero of equality. But we must be clear what "equality" means. It means "equality of rights," it means that every citizen of a state has the same rights. There must not be different laws for rich and poor, for the noble lord and the worker — that is what is meant by "equality" of rights. A hardworking person will, probably, get on better in life than a lazy one, but before the law, in a court case or in a legal argument they are equal.

But — only a hundred and fifty years ago — there existed people who, by the law of their country had no rights at all. They did not even have the right to leave their job if they did not like it. These people without rights were Negro slaves in the United States of America. In that great country that had rebelled against Britain over "rights" — the right to have a say in taxes — this great country still had black slaves in 1855.

Of course, some Americans said then that the slaves were well treated by most owners — they were not so badly off. But even if every slave owner had been kindness itself, slavery would still be wrong. And a good many slave owners were not kind but cruel and brutal — they could hurt and kill slaves as they pleased, for the slave had no rights.

Yet it was only the Southern states of the United States — Alabama, Georgia, Louisiana, the Carolinas, Virginia — which still allowed slavery. The reason why these Southern states still had Negro slaves was a plant which produces a white fluffy tuft — cotton.

Come to think of it, no plant has caused so much suffering as cotton: the conditions of the cotton mills of the Industrial Revolution in Britain, the slave trade in America. But, of course, it was not the plant, it was human greed which caused the suffering.

In the United States cotton could only be grown in the hot

climate of the Southern states, and the work in the vast cotton plantations was done by Negro slaves. In the North where cotton did not grow, there was no need for vast numbers of slaves. And so the Northern states, one after another, abolished slavery and set their Negroes free.

So in the middle of the nineteenth century then, the United States was a nation divided by the question of slavery. The Northern states had abolished slavery; it was against the law to have slaves. But the people of the Southern states said: "It is easy for you, you have no cotton plantations. But we in the South depend on cotton, and it would be quite impossible to work the cotton plantations and make a profit from them, without having Negro slaves to work them."

This state of things could go on — but only for a time. More and more people in the North felt it was wrong for a civilized nation, like the United States, to still have slaves like the ancient Romans, so they demanded that the Southern states should abolish slavery. In a modern country all men must have equal rights. The American Government in Washington should make a law for the whole of America that there should be no more slaves. As the Northern states had a majority in the Government, they could make such a law for the whole country.

But the Southern states said: "If you make such a law, then we shall break up the United States, and we, the Southern states will declare our part of America a separate country. We shall have a republic of our own and our own government, and keep the slaves." To which the Northern states replied: "We will not allow you to divide America. We shall keep you by force under the Government in Washington which is your and our Government."

That was the position in the year 1860. In that year Abraham Lincoln (1809–65) became President of the United States — that is the lawful President of the North and the South.

Abraham Lincoln's career was a typically American success story. He came from a very poor home in Kentucky which, at that time was still half wild. His mother died when he was only eight years old. His father was a carpenter, a restless man who cared little for his son. From the age of nine young Lincoln had to earn his own living — working on farms, working in shops or

helping on a ferry boat. In between these jobs he would occa-
sionally go to school. It wasn't his fault that he could not get a
proper education, but he tried to make up for it by educating
himself. When he was a shop assistant customers found him
with a book on the counter which he studied at every possible
moment.

Later on Lincoln started a small business, a shop, together
with a partner. But the partner was dishonest and a drunkard.
He drank himself to death and left Lincoln with enormous
debts. It took Lincoln many years to pay off these debts — but
pay he did. He was determined to be honest in all his dealings.

And in these years when he worked in shops and had to pay
these debts he began to study law in his spare time. And eventually, he passed his exams and became a lawyer in Springfield, the
capital of Illinois.

As a lawyer, Abraham Lincoln remained scrupulously honest. One day a man came to him with the request to take his case
to court. Lincoln listened to the man's story and then he said:
"Yes, I could take your case to court, I could win it and so get
from you five hundred dollar as my fee — but I won't do it,
because you are in the wrong. Goodbye."

With such a strong sense of fairness and justice Abraham
Lincoln had been against slavery from his youth. He thought it
was an evil that should disappear from America. He entered politics to fight this evil and was elected by the people of Springfield to be their Congressman in Washington. From there one
thing led to another, and in 1860, in that time of great tension,
Abraham Lincoln, the son of a poor carpenter, became President
of the United States.

Lincoln did not want to see his country split by a civil war,
and he promised not to force the Southern states to give up their
slaves. But they did not believe him and in January 1861 the
states South Carolina, Mississippi, Florida, Alabama, Georgia,
Louisiana and Texas declared themselves an independent republic and set up their own government (by May they were joined
by Virginia, Arkansas, Tennessee and North Carolina). They
also declared that "slavery was the natural condition of the
Negro."

This was open revolt, it was rebellion against the lawful government in Washington, and Abraham Lincoln as President had a duty to fight the rebels.

And so, in 1861, the terrible Civil War between the Southern states (the Confederates) and Northern states (the Unionists) began, a war in which people of the same nation fought each other, a war that lasted four years and in which six hundred thousand men lost their lives.

To begin with it was not a war to set the slaves free, it was a war to keep the Southern states in the Union, but during the war Abraham Lincoln declared that, if the North was going to win, then slavery in the South would be abolished.

In 1865 the war ended with the victory of the Northern states — and slavery came to an end in America. It would have been a blessing if fair-minded Abraham Lincoln had remained leader in peace as he had been in war. His aim was to treat the defeated Southern states not as conquered enemies, but as friends and so heal the wounds of war. But it was not to be so. Just before the surrender of the South, Lincoln went to a theatre one evening . A fanatical, half-mad Southerner made his way to the President's box during the performance, and shot him.

The President who came after Lincoln, Andrew Johnston, was unable to go against Congress which made the Southern states feel they were conquered enemies and so created a bitterness which lingered on in the South for many years.

The Negroes were no longer slaves, but this was only the beginning of the road to true equality. It took more than another hundred years for the Negroes to enjoy full equality of rights in America, especially in the South.

So around the same time as the Industrial Revolution in Britain brought demands for fraternity, and when in Europe, in Italy, there was a struggle for liberty, in America the Civil War was a war for equality. And the hero of this war for equality was Abraham Lincoln.

48. Tsar Alexander II

By a strange coincidence, at the time when there was a struggle for human rights and equality in America, the same kind of struggle took place in Russia, a country which became America's opponent in the second half of the twentieth century. At the time of the struggle between North and South in America, Russia, too, was coming to grips with the problem of equality.

Russia too, had at that time, its own kind of "slaves" — but they were called "serfs." The serfs in Russia were of Russian origin like their masters, but their life was as bad and miserable as that of any black slave in America.

At that time there were only a few cities in Russia, there were practically no industries, no factories, and most of this vast country was farmland. But there were no farmers as you find in Britain today. There were only vast estates — each stretching over thousands of acres — and these great estates were owned by the Russian aristocrats.

The workers, the peasants, who worked in the fields for their noble masters, were not "tenants" as they had been in Britain, they were "serfs" which meant they were the property of the owner, just like the cattle or the houses on the estate. But they were not just slaves. There was one difference. A slave in America could be sold on his own. A serf in Russia could only be sold if the land on which he lived was also being sold. The serfs were a part of the land, like the trees that grew on it.

The estate-owner gave his serfs neither money nor food. Each serf-family had a little plot of land to grow their own food — and they were supposed to work two days a week at their own plot — and four days a week in the fields of their master. But, in practice, the nobleman hardly ever gave them enough time for their own plots — and the serfs hardly ever had enough to eat.

The master could inflict any punishment he liked on his

serfs — for good reasons or for no reason at all. A thousand strokes with a birch rod was quite common. But there was one punishment the serfs feared more than any other. If a serf had shown disobedience several times he was sent to Siberia. There, where the ground was frozen nine months of the year, where millions of mosquitoes made life a misery in the warm months, there were the dreaded punishment or prison camps where the poor wretches, dressed in their rags even in the iciest cold and fed on a little bread and water worked until death came as a relief.

One quarter of the whole population of Russia were serfs — and this quarter worked and produced food for all the others.

Schools and universities existed only for the sons of the great land-owners and rich merchants. But what was taught in these schools and universities was laid down by the Government, by the Tsar of Russia and his ministers.

In Russia, too, the Tsar and the noblemen were afraid that the ideas of the French Revolution, the ideas of liberty, fraternity and equality, would spread and the people rise in revolt. And so that Government did everything possible to prevent the spreading of "dangerous" ideas.

In addition to the police who would arrest anybody who said or wrote anything dangerous or anti-government, there was also a secret police. The secret police were people who were paid by the Government to spy on everybody and to report anyone who showed by a careless word that he had "dangerous" ideas. Not even a high-ranking nobleman was safe from the secret police, and everybody in Russia, from prince down to serf, lived in fear of these spies. Once a spy of the secret police had reported you, you were doomed. There was no trial, no hearing in court, you were arrested and either executed or sent to the prison camps of Siberia to die a lingering death.

In 1855 a new Tsar came to the throne of Russia, Alexander II (1818–81). He was a man who wanted some progress in Russia. There was a new wind blowing in Russia — and the first sign of this new wind was that Alexander II, the new Tsar, gave permission for the building of railways in Russia. His father, the Tsar before him, had forbidden railways on the grounds that they would encourage unnecessary travelling and so make people restless.

The new Tsar, Alexander II, not only wanted railways, he wanted a very great change: he wanted to abolish serfdom, he wanted the serfs to become free and to have equal rights with the other people of Russia.

You might think that the serfs were pleased to hear the news that they were to be free. But they were not; as long as they were serfs they had at least a little plot of land given to them by their master. But if there were no longer serfs they would no longer have land, and such a life was no use. They would sooner remain serfs than be without land.

Alexander II realized that he would have to take land from the noblemen and give it to the peasants, but the noblemen had to be paid for this land. Who should pay for it? The peasants, of course. They should work the new plots given to them and sell a part of their crops, then year after year, pay a sum to the noblemen until they had paid for their land. This was a solution that seemed fair to both noblemen and serfs, and so serfdom was abolished in Russia.

The year 1861 is a great one for human rights in history. It was the year when the American Civil War began which led to slavery being abolished, and it was the year Tsar Alexander II abolished serfdom in Russia. It was a great step towards equality when in 1861, slavery in America, and serfdom in Russia were abolished.

Alexander II had done something for equality, for human rights, but he had no intention to allow the Russian people to have a say in government. He had absolute power and would not share it with a parliament. By then there were many people in Russia who wanted more freedom, specially the students at the universities. The students held public meetings in which they demanded elections and a parliament for Russia. The result was that hundreds of students were arrested and sent to Siberia.

Moreover, Tsar Alexander II decided that it was science in particular that made people think and get dangerous ideas in their heads, and so the teaching of science — physics, chemistry, physiology, astronomy — was simply forbidden. The only subjects which remained were Latin and Greek, history and geography.

The students hit back by making several attempts to kill Tsar Alexander II. He escaped and gave the secret police more power than they ever had before. The secret police could arrest, hang, shoot, or send anybody to Siberia, as they pleased. By now the students were determined that this tyrant of a Tsar should die. In 1881 Alexander II was being driven in a coach through the streets of Moscow when a student suddenly threw a bomb into the coach; it exploded and killed the Tsar.

Alexander II died because he had not realized that equality alone was not enough but that liberty, too, is necessary in the modern age. It is a strange coincidence that both the man who ended serfdom and the man who ended slavery were assassinated by political enemies.

49. Bismark

We have seen some of the great changes which took place in the nineteenth century, in Britain, and Italy, in France (where Napoleon III came to power), in America and in Russia. Now we come to Germany.

In the middle of the nineteenth century, Germany was — like Italy — not one country, but divided into many states each with its own ruler, though the people all spoke the same language. There was the Kingdom of Prussia, the Kingdom of Bavaria, the Kingdom of Saxony and many other smaller and larger states.

Just as in Italy, the people in Germany had a desire to become one united nation, but the different kings had no wish to give up their power. And when, in that "red" year of 1848, revolutions erupted in several parts of Germany, these uprisings were suppressed, and Germany remained divided.

Germany was not so fortunate as Italy, while there were freedom-loving people in Germany, there was no great leader like Garibaldi. And when Germany was united in the end, it was not the work of a man who loved freedom. Otto von Bismarck (1815–98), the man who formed Germany into one nation, was not interested in freedom, but in power.

Bismarck, born in 1815, was not the son of a poor family as Garibaldi was. His family were Prussian aristocrats, noblemen who had been great lords in Prussia since the Middle Ages. Bismarck was never a common sailor like Garibaldi, a shop assistant like Lincoln or Robert Owen; he grew up as the son of great land owners — and although the peasants on the estates were not serfs or slaves, they were still obedient and respectful to their masters. So young Bismarck grew up with the conviction that the world was made for masters who command, and servants who obeyed. Words like liberty, equality and fraternity meant nothing to him.

But young Bismarck was a clever boy, so clever that he did

well at school without working hard. It was the same at university: he spent most of his time fighting duels (sabre-fighting was a favourite sport amongst German students) and enjoying himself, yet he did very well at his exams.

The family was rich, so there was no need for Bismarck to work for a living, and he could settle down to the pleasant life of a great land-owner. But Bismarck was also a man of great energy — and doing nothing did not suit him at all, so he took an interest in the politics of his country, Prussia.

At this time the King of Prussia had already made some concessions to the people: he had allowed them to have a parliament. This parliament did not have much power, it could never go against the King, but it was at least some kind of democratic institution.

Bismarck became a member of this parliament. But he already had certain ideas about the future of Prussia and the future of Germany — and the parliament was, for him, only a means to achieve what he had in mind.

Bismarck agreed with the people who wanted the separate states of Germany to become united in one great nation, and he realized that such a united Germany could be a very powerful nation, a nation of many millions, a nation with the largest army in Europe. This united Germany could become one of the great world powers.

But how could Germany become united? Not by revolutions — a man like Bismarck, a nobleman, only had contempt for rebels and revolutions. No, there was another way. His own country, Prussia should force the other states of Germany to accept Prussia as master, and his own King, the King of Prussia, should become Emperor of Germany, of the whole nation. Not a revolution from below, but force from above should make Germany one nation.

We saw that 1861 was a fateful year in history. It was the year in which the Civil War that abolished slavery in America began, and when the serfs in Russia were set free, it was the year in which Italy became one nation under King Victor Emmanuel. It was also the year in which Bismarck became Prime Minister of Prussia and so could begin to put his ideas into practice.

To make Prussia strong enough to impose her will on the rest of Germany, she needed a large army, and such an army cost money. Bismarck asked the Prussian Parliament to increase taxes to pay for the army. In his speech he spoke words which were, unfortunately, prophetic. He said: "The great issues of the world will not be decided by words and arguments, but by blood and iron."

But the Prussian members of parliament thought the taxes were already high enough and voted against the increase — they knew that the people did not want to pay more taxes. But Bismarck was not interested in what the people wanted — he knew what he himself wanted: a large, strong Prussian army. He went to the King of Prussia and the King simply ordered that the taxes be put up. And the Prussians obeyed and paid.

So the Prussian army grew, it became the strongest, best-trained army within the German states, and the other states, Bavaria, Saxony did not like it at all — they had some idea what all this was about. But they all pinned their hopes on the country south of Germany: Austria. They hoped Austria was great enough and strong enough to stop Prussia from becoming master of Germany. They soon lost this hope.

In 1866 out of the blue and for very little reason, Bismarck started a war against Austria. After a shattering defeat, Austria begged for peace. The war was over in one month and Bismarck had shown the German states that none of them could hope to resist the Prussian army.

There was still one great power to the west of Germany which could interfere with Bismarck's plans: France under the Emperor Napoleon III. Bismarck wanted a war with France, but he wanted France to declare the war to make it appear that Prussia was only defending herself.

And he managed it. First he falsified a message Napoleon III had sent to the Prussian King, so that it seemed as if this message was a French insult to Prussia. Of course, the Prussian newspapers printed fiery articles against the French, and the French newspapers answered by writing wildly against the Prussians. Newspapers had (and still have) the power to sway people's minds. In France and in Prussia people became convinced that the "national honour" was at stake, hatred between the two nations grew, and in the end, Napoleon III did exactly what Bismarck had wanted him to do, he declared war on Prussia.

The war lasted two years, 1870–71 and ended, as Bismarck had foreseen, with the victory of the Prussians. In Paris a revolution broke out, Napoleon III had to flee and ended his days in England. France became a republic again.

But while the Prussian troops were in Paris, Bismarck and the King of Prussia had made their quarters in the great palace of Versailles, once built as the pride of the *Roi Soleil*, Louis XV.

And while they were at Versailles — the rulers of all the German states, the Kings of Bavaria and Saxony and all the others were called to Versailles and they came and did what they were expected to do: William, the King of Prussia was proclaimed ruler over the whole of Germany, Emperor of Germany. So it was in 1871, at Versailles, that Germany was united under Prussian rule. Bismarck had achieved his aim.

Italy was united in 1861, Germany ten years later in 1871, but it happened quite differently. Italy was united by a popular movement, by freedom fighters like Garibaldi. Germany was united by the ruthless scheming and planning of a man who cared little for freedom, Otto von Bismarck.

Up to the time of Bismarck, the Germans had little interest in power; they had produced thinkers, scientists, poets rather than great generals. But Bismarck pushed them in a new direction: he gave them a new ambition: to become a world power. It was the wrong ambition for Germany to have. In the following century in two world wars she paid a terrible price for this ambition.

50. The Turn of the Century

In the period from the end of the nineteenth to the beginning of the twentieth century there was what is sometimes called the second Industrial Revolution. From about 1880 onwards there was another great step forward which changed people's lives as much as or more than the first Industrial Revolution.

The second Industrial Revolution was brought about by the introduction of two things: electricity and petrol.

With electricity, there came the possibility to send power over long distances through cables, so that the power station can be miles away from the house where electric light or heat is used. All that is required is a wire carrying the current from the station to the house.

And as the current can also be used for sound there came the telegraph and the telephone. Imagine how these things changed life. Thomas Edison invented the light bulb in 1879 — now one could have light at a turn of a switch. With the telegraph which became popular in the 1840s, a written message could go across great distances in a few hours (taking down and repeating the message took the time). The telephone was invented by Alexander Graham Bell in 1876 and soon people could hear each other's voices over thousands of miles.

And petrol came as a new source of power besides coal and steam. With the invention of the petrol engine by Karl Benz in 1885 came cars and vans and lorries, motor boats and aeroplanes. And the aeroplane made travelling faster than people had ever dreamed possible.

Now take just three things together: telegraph (which was used like e-mail is today), telephone and aeroplane: they reduce distance. For an e-mail or a telephone call the distance from here to Australia is of no consequence. And by plane you can be in Australia in twenty-four hours.

In ancient times the distance, let us say, between the Rome of the Caesars and China was so great that the Romans did not even know China existed, and the Chinese did not know about Rome. Nowadays you could telephone from Rome to Beijing, or fly the distance in a day. The earth has become small, distances have shrunk — that was the result of the second Industrial Revolution.

But the question is, have the nations of the world really come nearer to each other in heart and soul through all this?

We shall deal with this question by analysing what happened between the nations of the world while this second Industrial Revolution took place.

To understand what happened, we must go back a few centuries, right back to Columbus, Pizarro, and Magellan, to the time of the great voyages. That was the time when Spain and Portugal were the first European nations to have colonies overseas. What was it that the Spaniards wanted most from their colonies? Gold, silver, treasure. And that was, for centuries, the only reason to have colonies. As long as they thought there was no gold there, the British Government was not even interested in Cook's discovery of Australia. It was just a place to send hardened criminals to.

But this simple idea of colonies had already changed with the first Industrial Revolution — for Britain with its cotton mills — a colony which grew cotton was not just useful — it was very important. And at the time of the second Industrial Revolution other things became important: copper for electrical cable, aluminium for planes, and of course, crude oil for petrol and diesel.

The British, having been the first in the Industrial Revolution, were also the first to realize that there was wealth in colonies even if they did not have a scrap of gold or silver. And so Britain grabbed colonies where she could, specially in Africa; you never knew what special produce could be found or discovered that might one day become valuable.

Of course, if there was a region in the world which did produce gold or diamonds — this too was to be taken, as you will see from the following story.

In 1870, in the year Bismarck started the war between Prussia and France that ended with the defeat of France and with Germany becoming one nation, in that year a young Englishman, Cecil Rhodes, arrived in South Africa. Rhodes was an office clerk with very little education and very little money. He only came to South Africa because he had lung trouble, and the doctors had told him that the damp climate of Britain was bad for him; he should go to a dry, sunny climate, and so he went to South Africa. Rhodes, though he was not well educated, was clever, and he had that special cleverness that makes a good businessman. Shortly after his arrival in South Africa the first diamonds were found at Kimberly.

A "prospector" who had found a few diamonds and "registered his claim" had the right to mine on the little plot of land which he had registered. But such a prospector was never rich enough to buy machines or pay workers to mine deeper than three or four metres, and so he would sell his claim for a few hundred pounds and go on to look for more. And the man who went straight to Kimberly and bought dozens and dozens of these claims was Rhodes. He did not even have the money to buy, he borrowed the money. He took great risks for some plots he bought contained only a few tiny diamonds. He might have lost on his deals — but he did not.

As he now owned large areas he could get machinery to pump the water out the ever deeper holes and employ hundreds of men to continue digging deeper to find more diamonds. He could easily repay the borrowed money with interest and still have a fortune.

These diamond-mines were in the British Cape Colony. But there were also two independent Boer Republics in South Africa, the Transvaal and the Orange Free State. The Boers were descendants of Dutch settlers.

It happened that gold was found in the Boer Republic of Transvaal, at Johannesburg. And thousands of British prospectors and adventurers poured into the Boer Republic in search for gold. The Boers did not like this invasion — there was no end of trouble. Cecil Rhodes, who was by now a rich and very respected man, thought that the riches of Johannesburg should become British — the whole of South Africa should become British. At first he equipped — at his own expense — a little army and sent it into the Boer country, but the Boers drove the invaders out. And then Cecil Rhodes went to England, persuaded the British Government to make war against the Boers and to take possession of their lands.

And so in 1899 the Boer War started. With the British troops fighting against the Boers was a young English journalist, Winston Churchill, who had come to send reports and description of the battles to his newspaper in London. Being a journalist and not a soldier, Churchill should (like a Red Cross worker) not have taken part in fighting, nor should he have carried any weapon. But young Churchill did not much bother about rules and carried a revolver on him although he knew that if the Boers caught him and found the gun, they could shoot him for breaking the rules.

One day Churchill travelled with two companies of British troops in a train. Suddenly the train stopped with a crash and bullets came whistling through the windows, the train had run into a Boer ambush. The British found themselves surrounded on all sides by Boers and surrendered. Churchill too was taken prisoner and was brought before a Boer officer. At his command Churchill was searched and the revolver was found. The Boer officer would have been within his rights to have Churchill shot, but he took pity on the young man and spared his life. Churchill was sent to a prison camp.

Three weeks later Churchill escaped. But he was in enemy country, knew no word of their language and had no money. His only hope was to get out of the Boer country to a Portuguese colony in Africa. To get there he got into an empty truck on a train rolling in the right direction. All night he travelled, but in the morning the train rolled to a stop and Churchill quickly jumped off before he was discovered. He came to a farm and was lucky, for the farmer was English and kept him hidden for weeks in a rat-infested coal mine. At long last it was safe for Churchill to get into another empty truck on a train and, eventually, he came safely out of the Boer Republic and into the neutral Portuguese Colony. Four weeks later he was back with the British troops, but this time as an officer and to fight.

After a long and bitter struggle, the Boers lost the war, and their country became a British colony. Many years later South Africa became a dominion — it remained British but had its own Prime Minister. The name of this first Prime Minister of South Africa was Jan Smuts, and he was the officer who had spared Churchill's life. He and Churchill became great friends and were allies in the two world wars that came.

For many years in South Africa, however, the Boers did not forgive the British for taking their country by force of arms.

51. The First World War

By the end of the nineteenth century, colonies became important for other products than gold, silver or diamonds; now copper, rubber, and oil were needed by the second Industrial Revolution. But there were other products too: coffee and tea became popular in Europe and a colony that produced coffee or tea was valuable.

Marie Curie, a scientist, discovered a new element which no one had known existed, radium, which became much more valuable than gold. Radium is used for cancer treatment and used to be applied to watch numerals, as it shines in the dark (it was later found that this radioactive element was very dangerous to health, and so it is no longer used for watches). Some other rare metals, wolfram, tungsten, were found to be important for steel production, and aluminium, of which no one had taken notice before, became a metal much in demand, as it was strong and light.

All these new things required by the second Industrial Revolution needed had to come from overseas, because they could not be found readily in Europe. As other countries in Europe became industrialized, they too wanted colonies to get all these raw materials. And, so other European nations rushed to claim what was still there for claiming. France took large slices of north and west Africa and Indo-China, Germany got hold of parts of east and west Africa, Belgium got hold of a part of Central Africa, and Holland strengthened her hold on the Indonesian islands (Java, Sumatra) in Asia. In short, it was like a race, with everyone trying to catch up with Britain.

It was the Industrial Revolution that was the driving force behind this grabbing of colonies, the Industrial Revolution with its need for all kinds of new raw materials.

Britain had been the first in this race for colonies, with France following behind, and some way farther back came Germany.

The British Government was not very pleased with all the other countries doing what the British had done. For nearly a century Britain had the largest colonial empire in the world. And Britain had also built up the greatest navy in the world. Now other nations not only acquired colonies and built large navies, becoming competitors, and a threat to Britain's wealth and power. Britain regarded Germany as a more dangerous threat than France.

Ever since Bismarck's time, the Germans had continued to build up a strong army. German industries in the Ruhr and elsewhere were soon larger than Britain's, German colonies had been established in Africa, and then under Emperor William II, Germany began to build up a navy that might one day equal that of Britain.

Not only did the British Government regard Germany as a danger, but France too (still smarting since the lost war of 1870–71) feared the growing power of Germany, and the Tsar of Russia was afraid that Germany might attack her with her great army.

And so Britain, France and Russia formed a great alliance, the *Entente Cordiale,* agreeing that if any one of them was attacked, the others would come to that country's aid. Of course, the name of Germany was not even mentioned in this agreement, but they had no doubt who was meant.

But now the Germans felt threatened by this great alliance against them — they saw themselves threatened from east and west and north. But the Germans on their part also found an ally in the Austro-Hungarian Empire.

And so, from the early years of this century onwards, there were two major powers in Europe; Britain, France, Russia on one side, Germany and Austria on the other. And in all these countries armies were strengthened and enlarged, navies were built up, and Europe became increasingly like a powder keg that just needed a spark to explode.

The spark came in 1914. The Crown Prince of Austria, the heir to the Austrian throne, was assassinated in Sarajevo. The murderer escaped to neighbouring Serbia. The Austrians demanded that the murderer should be handed over to them,

and while the Serbian Government hesitated, the Austrian army
marched into Serbia. But Serbia had an alliance with Russia, and
so Russia declared war on Austria.

And now all the other alliances came in: Germany had to
help Austria and declared war on Russia; France and Britain
declared war on Germany and Austria, and so the First World
War started. It became, indeed, a world war because it was
fought not only in Europe, but in the colonies as well — the
British and French colonies sent troops to the battlefields of
Europe. It was a world war because, in the end, America, too,
came in on the side of Britain and against Germany.

It was a terrible war — never before had human lives been
sacrificed in war in such large numbers. In the two-day Battle of
Passchendaele alone over half a million men were lost — and
still the war went on. It was during this terrible First World War
that aeroplanes were used for the first time, and for the first time
tanks went into action. For the first time submarines attacked
surface ships, and for the first time poison gas was used.

One could say, that in the First World War, the Industrial
Revolution came to the armies and to the battlefield. What
Leonardo da Vinci had feared: that machines would make war
more terrible, became true in the First World War.

Finally the First World War ended with the defeat of
Germany and Austria in 1918. But before the end, while
Germany was still fighting on, something happened which was,
perhaps more important than the whole war. In 1917 Germany
and Austria were still fighting on but already exhausted. Was
there any way in which they could knock out at least one of their
enemies, Russia? There was one way: causing a revolution. If
there was a revolution against the Tsar in Russia, and civil war,
the Russians would fight each other instead of Germany.

The Russians hated the Tsar Nicholas who had plunged
Russia into war that had already cost the lives of two million
Russians. They hated the Tsar who would not allow more freedom, and, in fact, the Tsar was forced by his own generals to
abdicate and a democratic government took over. But this new
government continued the war against Germany.

And now the Germans had to think how to start another revolution in Russia, a revolution against this democratic Government.

There were two Russians living in Switzerland who were the leaders of the Russian Communists, followers of Karl Marx. Their names were Lenin (Vladimir Ilyitch Ulianov was his real name) and Trotsky. They had both fled from Russia before the War, but they were secretly in contact with fellow-Communists inside Russia.

What the German generals thought was this: if we get Lenin and his friend Trotsky back to Russia, they will start a Communist revolution, and that will stop the Russians fighting against Germany.

And this was what really happened; Lenin could not have gone to Russia without going through Germany; he could never have gone through Germany without the permission of the German Generals. It was the German Generals who offered Lenin and Trotsky a free passage through Germany to the Russian border. In sealed railway carriages the two Communist leaders passed through Germany and entered Russia via Finland in disguise. There they started the Communist revolution. Lenin promised peace, and the peasants, tired of war, followed him. On the night of November 6–7, 1917, the democratic government was thrown out by armed Communists, Lenin took power and Russia became the first Communist country in the world. The Tsar and his family were shot by the Communists.

Nevertheless, in the end, a year later, Germany and Austria lost the war. But without the help of the German generals, there may not have been a Communist Russia, Lenin would have stayed in Switzerland, and Russia may have become a democratic country.

That was, perhaps, the most important result of the First World War, that one of the greatest countries in the world became Communist. The other result was that Germany and Austria were defeated and the defeat brought great changes to these two countries.

52. The Rise of Nationalism

In the old days a war in Europe, let us say between France and Germany, meant conflict in Europe only. But with the Industrial Revolution came the need for raw materials and for colonies so any war in Europe also brought war in the colonies, and so became a world war.

This is the other side of the Industrial Revolution. While railways, steamships, aeroplanes, telegraph and telephone made distance unimportant and brought countries closer together as if the earth had shrunk, it also meant that any conflict in one spot could spread rapidly over the whole globe.

This is something people did not realize in 1914 when the First World War started, but it is high time that we know it and realize it. The modern means of communication have made the earth into one big village, and a fire that starts in one corner of that village can set all the huts aflame.

In the past people said that all mankind is one family, but it was just a beautiful idea. Today it is no longer an idea, it is a fact brought about by the means of communication. We are one family living in one village, called earth. It is a fact, not a hope or a dream.

Today the thought: "My nation comes first, and never mind all the others" is alien and two hundred or three hundred years in the past. Nationalism, which means wanting advantages for your own nation without caring if others suffer, in our time, is just as outdated as people still wandering around wearing suits of armour.

But, unfortunately, after the First World War, the world had not yet learned this lesson, its nations became not less but more nationalistic. They became more selfish as nations, and so nationalism — national selfishness — prepared the way for another catastrophe: the Second World War.

Let us take one example of blind, selfish nationalism.

Before the First World War, the Austro-Hungarian Empire was a union of several nationalities: there was one part where the people spoke German, there was one part where the people spoke Slavic languages, and another where the people spoke Hungarian, and there were still others. It was a great advantage to these small nationalities that they could live together in one great state and trade with each other. But in 1918 when Austria lost the First World War, revolutions broke out. The last Austrian Emperor had to flee, and instead of staying together in one great republic, each nationality set up their own republic and so came new states: Czechoslovakia, Hungary, Yugoslavia, Poland, and German-speaking Austria as it is today.

All these little states only came into existence in 1918 after the First World War. And they did not work together but against each other, they were nationalistic and jealous of each other.

Take another example that was even worse. Italy, the land of Garibaldi, had been in the First World War on the side of Britain and France, but the Italian soldiers had suffered many defeats from the Austrians, and Italy had no reason to be proud when the war ended. There was great poverty in the land and many Italian factory workers became Communists. And this frightened the Italian capitalists. They were afraid that Italy would become Communist, like Russia and they would lose their factories and estates, they would lose their wealth. And just then a man appeared who claimed he could save Italy from Communism; he was a journalist by profession, and his name was Benito Mussolini.

Mussolini claimed that democracy, parliament and freedom, had spoiled and ruined the Italian people — that Italy needed one strong man, one leader with absolute power, a dictator and that this dictator would make Italy a world power as ancient Rome had been. Of course this great leader could be no one else but Mussolini himself.

Mussolini as dictator would certainly not allow Communism, and so the capitalists of Italy supported him with large gifts of money. Mussolini used the money to arm and train a private army whose uniform was black —

Blackshirts. Garibaldi, the fighter for freedom, had given his men red shirts. Mussolini, the fighter against freedom, gave his men black shirts. And in 1922 Mussolini marched his army of thirty thousand Blackshirts into Rome, and forced the Italian Parliament to give him absolute power. Mussolini became Dictator of Italy.

As dictator Mussolini made an end of all political parties in Italy. All parties were forbidden, the party leaders were imprisoned, and specially the Communists were ruthlessly persecuted. No paper or book could appear which criticized the dictator. All newspapers had to praise Mussolini and all newspapers had to preach wild, fanatical nationalism. In all schools children had to be drilled to look up to Mussolini with awe and reverence, and the whole Italian nation was drilled to fight for him and for the glory of Italy, as the greatest nation in the world. It was nationalism gone mad.

It seems strange now, but Britain and France, were at first quite pleased with this enemy of freedom, the dictator Mussolini. After all, he kept the Communists down, and that was for the greater good. They did not realize that nationalism was a danger.

The example of Mussolini caught on in Germany. Germany had lost the First World War, she had lost her colonies, her soldiers had died in vain. The poverty was even worse than in Italy, and hundreds and thousands of workers were out of jobs. In Germany, too, the Emperor had been chased away and the country was ruled by a parliament, but this German Parliament could do nothing to help the poverty and the mass unemployment.

The victorious powers, Britain, France, America could have helped by giving Germany money, but they were too selfish, too nationalist, to help a former enemy. Quite the contrary, every year Germany had to pay large sums, millions of pounds, as a kind of punishment to the victorious nations.

It is no wonder that the German people became desperate, and that in their despair, they were willing to listen to a man who promised to become a German Mussolini, a great leader who would once again make Germany a great and powerful nation. The name of this German leader was Adolf Hitler.

If Mussolini's nationalism was mad, Hitler's brand of nationalism was an evil insanity. According to Hitler the Germans were chosen by destiny to be a master-race and to rule the world. All other races and nations in the world were inferior, in fact they were hardly human at all. A coloured race, like the Negroes, were according to Hitler, not better than animals and should be treated as such. But Hitler's special hatred and contempt was for the Jews, the Jews should be exterminated like vermin, like rats.

It seems strange that people could fall for these mad ideas, after all the German Jews had fought as soldiers in the German army like every other German. But the fact is that Hitler did gain a large following in Germany, and in 1933, eleven years after Mussolini, became Führer of Germany.

In Germany, too, any opinion that was opposed to Hitler was suppressed — newspapers and books preached only the idea that the Germans were superior to other nations and races and that Hitler was a genius who could never be wrong. Having lost the First World War Germany was preparing for a second one which, led by the genius Hitler, they thought they could not lose.

Not all Germans fell for Hitler's mad nationalism — there were thousands who recognized the evil — but anyone who spoke out openly was sent to the concentration camps — where inhuman conditions and cruel treatment brought a lingering death, so it was safer to keep silent. A number of Jews fled from Germany. Others, specially elderly people, stayed. They hoped Hitler would spare old people who could do no harm. They were mistaken.

Once Hitler had built up a vast army, he set out on his path of conquest. He was actually a born Austrian — and the first country he took was Austria (the German-speaking part was all that was left of the Austro-Hungarian Empire). There was no fighting — most Austrians were pleased; they thought it was a good thing to be a part of Hitler's Greater Germany. They were mistaken, but it was too late when they realized it.

Then Hitler and Mussolini, the two dictators, formed an alliance and the other European nations — Britain and France, but also the small nations, Czechoslovakia, Poland, Yugoslavia — realized that there was now a new and terrible power in Europe: a fanatical, mad nationalism led by ruthless dictators and in command of vast, well-armed and well-trained armies.

53. The Second World War

Britain and France were well aware that Hitler and Mussolini were getting ready for another war, but there were also people in the British Government who believed that Hitler would use his great armies to war against Russia only — against the Communists. And so they did nothing to stop him when he marched his armies into Czechoslovakia and took the Sudetenland, a large German-speaking slice of that country.

But Britain and France did warn Hitler that if he attacked any other country they would oppose him. Hitler was so certain that the British would not go to war that he ignored the warning and in 1939 German troops invaded Poland and conquered the country in a few days.

By now Britain and France knew that there could be no peace with Hitler, no peace with his mad nationalism. They declared war on Germany and so in 1939 the Second World War began.

At first the Germans won battle after battle — they conquered the whole of France; they struck North and took Norway by surprise. The cities of Britain were bombed night after night by the German air force.

It was in this dark and hopeless stage of the war that Winston Churchill became Prime Minister of Britain and kept the spirit of courage and defiance alive in the British people.

It needed great courage not to give in, for the Germans and Italians occupied the whole Balkan peninsula — Yugoslavia, Romania, Greece, and crossed over to North Africa. Only a small British army in Egypt stood against them. On the seas the German submarines attacked the convoys, the fleets of ships which brought food to Britain, and troops and arms from Britain to the colonies.

No one knows what would have happened if Hitler had decided to invade Britain. He was at the height of his power — except for Spain, and the neutral countries of Switzerland and

Sweden, the whole of the European continent was in his power — when he decided to attack Russia. In 1942 the German armies marched into Russia. And now history repeated itself. What had happened to Napoleon and his *Grande Armée* also happened to the German Armies.

They marched on and on, the Russian armies went back before them but destroyed all the crops. Only this time the German armies did not enter Moscow: at Moscow the Russians made a stand, and the Germans could not break through the Russian defence. Just like Napoleon's soldiers the German armies were caught by the terrible Russian Winter, and although they did not go back (as Napoleon had done), they suffered terrible losses in the Russian winter.

While all this happened in Europe, the Japanese, another ally of Hitler struck in the East. Out of the blue and without warning the Japanese air force attacked the American fleet at Pearl Harbour in Hawaii, sinking nearly all the American ships there. The Japanese then invaded the Philippines and went on to take the British colonies of Hong Kong, Malaya and Singapore, and the Dutch colonies, Java and Sumatra (which later became Indonesia).

However, now Britain was no longer alone, the two greatest world powers, America and Russia were on her side.

And Hitler, vast as the German army was, had not only to fight the Russians in the East, but to guard the whole coastline of Europe from Denmark to Greece, against a possible invasion from the sea.

And the invasion came, first in the Mediterranean. The British forces had driven the Germans from North Africa, and together with the Americans, they crossed over to Italy. In Italy a revolution against Mussolini broke out and eventually he was shot by his own people. The Germans still had armies in Italy, but they were finally driven back.

In the meantime, British and American air forces bombed Germany creating much worse destruction than the Germans had ever inflicted on Britain. Eventually in 1944, combined British and American forces under the American General Eisenhower invaded France.

Attacked from west and south and east, the German armies

fought on, but now the odds were against them. In 1945 the German war machines collapsed, and as the victorious Russians poured into Berlin, Hitler committed suicide in his bunker.

The other German leaders were brought before a court in Nuremberg. They were found guilty of having ordered the mass-murder of millions of civilians in concentration camps. Six million Jews had been exterminated, as well as Poles, Russians, and anti-Hitler Germans. Most of these leaders were hanged, others received long prison sentences.

Germany had suffered terribly in the war, her cities were rubble heaps, her sons lay on battlefields all over Europe, her industries were destroyed. That was the price Germany paid for nationalism.

But, unfortunately the victorious allies were soon quarrelling amongst themselves — Russian on one side, America, Britain, France on the other. The result of this quarrel was that the Russians made the eastern part of Germany they had occupied a Communist state (the German Democratic Republic), and the western part of Germany, which was occupied by American, British and French troops, became the Federal Republic of Germany with a parliament in Bonn. Berlin, in the middle of eastern Germany, was similarly divided, leaving an island of western Germany in the east.

For the next fifty years, until 1989, Germany remained divided into these two states.

When Hitler's power in Europe collapsed, the Japanese in Asia were still fighting on. No doubt, in time, Britain, America and Russia could have invaded Japan. But in the meantime scientists (some of them Jews who had fled from Hitler) in America had developed the most terrible weapon the world had ever known: the atom bomb. It was not necessary to invade Japan and lose the lives of thousands of American and British soldiers, one demonstration would make Japan surrender.

The demonstration came on August 9, 1945; on that day an atom bomb was dropped on Hiroshima and two days later another on Nagasaki. In a second these two cities were turned into rubble, tens of thousands of people were turned into dust so fine that it could not be seen, the glare of the explosion burned every eye that had seen it, and over the doomed cities rose the strange and terrible mushroom-shaped cloud.

There were people who survived the atom bomb explosion in Hiroshima and Nagasaki. But the terrible thing was that many died later, slow and painful deaths resulting from the radioactive fallout. And worse was to come — years later when these survivors had children, some were born blind, or without arms, or otherwise horribly damaged.

Japan surrendered, and the Second World War came to an end in 1945. Realizing that in a world that had become a village, wars were madness, the nations of the world set up a council to settle all disputes peacefully: the United Nations, the UN. What really came was neither peace nor war, but the so-called Cold War.

America, which believed in a free market and in everybody making as much money as possible, and Russia, which believed in Communism and control of all things by the state, had never trusted each other, not even when they were allies during the war. As soon as the war against Hitler was over, they quite openly became enemies.

At first the Americans thought that having the atom bomb made them stronger than Russia, that only the Americans knew how to make an atom bomb. But some scientists who had worked on the atom bomb were secretly Communists, and betraying the Americans, they gave the method of making atom bombs to the Russians.

Since then, America and Russia have both developed even more terrible bombs — each now having sufficient weaponry to kill all life on earth. And since then, many more countries have developed nuclear capabilities.

As long as there is nationalism, countries will not reach agreements to scrap these terrible weapons. But the Second World War has not only bequeathed us the atom bomb, but something else.

The people in the colonies were no longer willing to be under the rule of the white men. They demanded freedom, they demanded equality, fraternity, and Britain and France had to give up their colonies, one after another. The great colonial empires of the nineteenth century disappeared, and in their place came new independent states.

54. Prospects

In the fifty years following the Second World War, Cold War divided not only America and Russia but the whole world into two camps. On the one side the western countries — America, Britain, France, western Germany — believe in free enterprise, they believe that each person should be free to think as he likes, to work as he likes and to have as much property as he can acquire.

In the East, Russia and Poland and Yugoslavia, in China, there was the Communist system which believed that the whole community, the state should lay down what each person should think, how and where they should work and that no one should own property such as houses, factories, or land. Only the state, the whole community, could own property.

In the West, there is a stronger belief in freedom, in liberty, and people expect to have freedom in everything: in thinking, in writing, but also in business, in economics.

In the East, in the Communist countries there was a much greater feeling for brotherhood, for fraternity, for people working for the whole community. But they wanted this community in everything, not only in the work people did, but also in what they thought. And so, in the Communist countries, no book or newspaper could be printed, no teacher could teach, without the approval of the government.

The western countries, the capitalist countries as the Communists called them, put too many things in one basket called freedom. And the eastern countries, the Communist countries, put too many things in one basket called brotherhood, fraternity.

Today we can see two tendencies in the world. On the one hand countries are forming alliances, such as the European Union, usually beginning from an economic viewpoint, but then, as we have seen with Europe, spreading to all aspects of life.

On the other we see more and more countries slitting and falling apart, often violently, into fiercely nationalistic and ethnic groupings.

And there will be no peace and no real progress in the new states around the world until nationalism is recognized as something that does not belong to our time, and until liberty, equality, fraternity are each put in their right place in life.

Our own future will very much depend on how these questions are solved. No matter how well we do in our job, the world is only one big village and any spot of trouble or fighting in one corner can lead to a world-wide catastrophe, that destroys our work and our hopes. But by knowing the right place for liberty, the right place for equality and the right place for fraternity, we can contribute something towards a better world, a world in which children can grow up without the dark cloud of war and destruction hanging over them. Don't think that a single person can do nothing; it is not what Garibaldi thought, and not what Henri Dunant thought.

So we have come to the end of our history lessons. They started with the five sons of Pandu in ancient India,* and that was the time when men hardly felt at home on earth and longed to go back to heaven. Then in the Persian times gods still appeared in dreams and gave men their fine inventions, like the plough. We came then to the times of ancient Greece when the dreams disappeared and men began to think for themselves. Then there was the rise and fall of the Roman Empire — and that was the time when Jesus Christ told men that they were all brothers — sons of the Father in Heaven.

Then the warlike Germanic tribes destroyed the Roman Empire and set up new kingdoms, like the Angles and Saxons who came to Britain. These wild tribes became Christians — and their fighting spirit became tamed in the rules of knighthood.

The rise of Islam amongst the Arabs was followed with the wealth and power of Baghdad and the other Arab cities. And the Crusades, which failed to keep Jerusalem Christian, brought

* See C. Kovacs, *Ancient Mythology,* Wynstones Press.

new knowledge to Europe and made people curious about far-away lands. Spices became highly desirable and ships began to sail out to India, the land of spices. And so Columbus sailed West to reach India and, instead, discovered America.

Then followed Leonardo, the Renaissance genius, and Luther and the Reformation. Then came the wars of religion, and the Civil War in Britain between the Roundheads and Cavaliers, and in Scotland the last Stuart King, Bonnie Prince Charlie.

Then came the history of France — from the proud *Roi Soleil,* Louis XIV, to the French Revolution and Napoleon. That was the time when the ideas of liberty, equality, fraternity were introduced to mankind.

The Industrial Revolution, as it came step by step, made these three ideas even more important and more urgent.

"History" means the story of the *past,* it means speaking of things that happened either long ago or more recently. The overview of our past can help us gain a perspective on the future, the kind of history you will be living through in the next twenty, thirty, forty, years.

Index

Other Waldorf Education Resources
by Charles Kovacs

Class 4 (age 9–10)
Norse Mythology

Classes 4 and 5 (age 9–11)
The Human Being and the Animal World

Classes 5 and 6 (age 10–12)
Ancient Greece
Botany

Class 6 (age 11–12)
Ancient Rome

Classes 6 and 7 (age 11–13)
Geology and Astronomy

Class 7 (age 12–13)
The Age of Discovery

Classes 7 and 8 (age 12–14)
Muscles and Bones

Class 8 (age 13–14)
The Age of Revolution

Class 11 (age 16–17)
Parsifal and the Search for the Grail

General interest
The Spiritual Background to Christian Festivals